Opening Up the Suburbs

Opening Up the Suburbs

AN URBAN STRATEGY FOR AMERICA

Anthony Downs

New Haven and London

Yale University Press

Originally published with assistance from the foundation established in memory of
Amasa Stone Mather of the Class of 1907, Yale College.

Library of Congress catalog card number: 76-158984
International standard book number: 0-300-01464-3

Designed by John O. C. McCrillis
and set in Baskerville type.
Printed in the United States of America by
The Colonial Press Inc., Clinton, Massachusetts.

Published in Great Britain, Europe, and Africa by Yale University Press,
Ltd., London.
Distributed in Latin America by Kaiman & Polon, Inc., New York City; in
Australasia and Southeast Asia by John Wiley & Sons Australasia Pty. Ltd.,
Sydney; in India by UBS Publishers' Distributors Pvt., Ltd., Delhi; in Japan
by John Weatherhill, Inc., Tokyo.

Contents

Tables

Preface

"One nation . . . indivisible, with liberty and justice for all," says America's Pledge of Allegiance. In reality, our nation—like all others—contains many divisions, both good and bad. This book focuses upon counteracting the undesirable effects caused by one deeply entrenched division: the legal and political separation between central cities and suburbs in our metropolitan areas.

The most serious drawback of this division is exclusion of most poor, near-poor, and ethnic minority households from many of our suburban areas. Such exclusion helps perpetuate a host of problems by concentrating the burdens of coping with poverty inside central cities. It also prevents suburbs from achieving certain improvements in their efficiency and quality of life. Moreover, this exclusion will eventually undermine achievement of one of our fundamental goals: true equality of opportunity.

We have already recognized the un-American implications of suburban exclusion based upon race or nationality. But there is no correspondingly widespread recognition of the long-run drawbacks of excluding the poor and near-poor from suburbs. Therefore, this book focuses upon the need to open up the suburbs *economically* rather than *ethnically*, even though both are vital in the long run.

Specifically, throughout this book, "opening up the suburbs" means increasing housing opportunities in all *suburban areas for low-income households and in* new-growth *portions* of *suburban areas for moderate-income households.* I define "low-income households" as those with incomes below the officially defined "poverty line," and "moderate-income households" as those with incomes above the poverty line but below the national median. In 1970, the officially defined poverty line for a four-person nonfarm household was $3,968, and 25.5 million Americans

(13 percent of the total population) were officially defined as "poor." The 1970 median family income was $9,870. Since 50 percent of the population have incomes below the median, 37 percent (50 minus 13) had "moderate incomes" in 1970 by my definition.[1]

The word *suburbs* refers to all parts of all metropolitan areas outside of central cities. It therefore includes unincorporated areas as well as suburban municipalities. This usage reflects the way the United States Bureau of the Census tabulates information for a wide range of variables. It admittedly ignores the enormous diversity of characteristics among the nation's 18,000 suburbs.[2]

The issues in this book are among the most important, complex, controversial, and baffling facing American society. Understanding them is doubly difficult because both advocates and opponents of opening up the suburbs claim their adversaries' arguments are not really legitimate. In contrast, I believe both positions are based upon legitimate desires to achieve valid objectives. I have therefore tried to suggest policies that will help both sides to attain their objectives. However, I do not pretend to have developed any definitive or final resolution of the issues concerned. Since these issues are crucial to the future quality of life in American society, my goal is to expose at least some ideas about them that are important but not widely known. I hope these ideas will stimulate further thought, analysis, and research on the subject.

In presenting this book, I play three partly overlapping roles. The one predominant in most of the book is that of a social scientist. The second role is that of an advocate proposing certain goals and policies that I believe society should adopt and advancing arguments favoring them. I have tried to set forth the main arguments against these goals and policies, too, and to evaluate them objectively. The third role is that of an adviser or "consultant" to society. My purpose here is to confront society with the values and consequences implicit in its existing behavior and to pose alternatives for consideration.

This book started as an "instant translation" of a 1971 Yale lecture series presented at the suggestion of Joel Fleishman. It gradually burgeoned into a longer, more complex, and very different volume, but I have since condensed it into this essay, risking oversimplification to make its contents more widely accessible. As always, I have benefited greatly from the insights of my colleagues at Real Estate Research Corporation. However, the ideas in this book do not necessarily represent the views of the corporation, any of its clients, or any affiliated organizations. I am especially grateful to Leanne Lachman, Fran Sontag, James Q. Wilson, Antonia Chayes, and John McKnight for their excellent advice. Other members of the urban analysis profession from whom I have stolen or borrowed ideas are too numerous to mention.

This book is dedicated to my five children—Kathy, Christine, Tony, Paul, and Carol. Writing it deprived them of my presence all too often; and they will inherit the lifelong challenge of coping with the issues it involves.

A. D.

Chicago, Illinois
March 1973

1 Urban Development in the United States and Its Inherent Injustice

Urban development in America is frequently described as "chaotic" and "unplanned" because it produces what many critics call "urban sprawl." But economically, politically, and socially, American urban development occurs in a systematic, highly predictable manner. It leads to precisely the results desired by those who dominate it. As a consequence, most urban households with incomes above the national median or somewhat lower enjoy relatively high quality neighborhood environments.

Yet this process is also inherently unjust to millions of other American households. Furthermore, it contributes to rising maladies in many central cities, including high crime rates, vandalism, housing abandonment, low quality schools, and fiscal difficulties.

Unfortunately, most Americans do not understand how these ills are partly caused by the very process that has helped them achieve good quality neighborhoods. Until they realize what really happens in American urban development, they will not see why we need to open up the suburbs. This chapter seeks to provide such an understanding.

THE WORLDWIDE ECONOMICS OF URBAN DEVELOPMENT

Throughout the world, new urban development occurs mainly on vacant land around the fringes of built-up areas. This happens because the rate of return on private and public investment in new buildings and other improvements is much higher there than elsewhere. Hence, the "natural" forces of urban land markets generate the basic "inside-outward" pattern of urban growth found almost everywhere in the world.

In most growing urban areas, all income groups simultaneously increase in population. Therefore, they all require more housing and other urban facilities. Where there are no constraints on the quality of new housing, new-growth areas around the urban periphery respond to these needs by adding accommodations for all income groups. The poorest households build their own new housing—usually shacks—on land they have expropriated. Wealthy and middle-income groups build much higher quality housing on land they have bought. Wealthier households deliberately exclude the poorest people from their neighborhoods through laws requiring high quality housing plus police prevention of land expropriation. But either there are no area-wide prohibitions against the creation of new low quality housing, or such prohibitions are largely ignored by local authorities. Therefore, thousands of the very poorest households live around the urban periphery along with much wealthier households.

Poor households also occupy deteriorated housing found in older neighborhoods near the center of each urban area. But some of the oldest central neighborhoods are still occupied by the wealthy, who have kept older dwellings in excellent condition (as in Paris or London). Thus there is no area-wide separation of the poorest and wealthiest households on the basis of distance from the center of urbanization. Very poor and very wealthy neighborhoods—and a variety in between— are present in both older central districts and brand-new peripheral growth areas. This pattern of urban development can be seen clearly in cities like Caracas, Lagos, Manila, Rio de Janeiro, Accra, and Bombay.

THE AMERICAN "TRICKLE-DOWN" PROCESS

In the United States, this "natural" pattern of development is hindered by ubiquitous laws against creating or maintaining low quality housing and by differential enforcement of those laws by zones within each metropolitan area. The American economy has succeeded in raising living standards remarkably high for large portions of the population. This has led to widespread acceptance of two ideas central to American urban development but rarely discussed openly.

The first is that every American household ought to live in a decent housing unit—regardless of whether it can afford to do so with its own income. This idea has become official federal policy, as stated in the Housing Acts of 1949 and 1968, which called for "Realization as soon as feasible . . . of a decent home and a suitable living environment for every American family."

The second idea is that the minimum housing quality considered "decent" should be derived from prevalent middle-class or upper-middle-class living standards. These two ideas have become institutionalized in both building codes and housing codes. In most urban areas in the United States, building codes make it illegal to create a new low quality housing unit (except for a mobile home).[1] And housing codes make it illegal to occupy or maintain any low quality housing unit, new or old. At the same time, the costs of creating any new housing unit of the minimum quality legally allowed are very high.

As a result, nearly all new housing units in the United States (again excepting mobile homes) are too expensive for low- and moderate-income households to occupy—and even for many middle-income households. There is nothing "natural" about this condition. Rather it results from legally preventing landowners from building whatever types of new dwelling units they desire on their land. But it has profound consequences for the entire urban development process. These consequences can best be understood by tracing the history of a typical newly built neighborhood as it goes through the "filtering" or "trickle-down" process.

When first created, the new neighborhood contains a cluster of housing units of basically similar quality, style, and price level. They were all built by a single developer or group of developers appealing to about the same market. The neighborhood is initially located near the edge of existing settlement in its metropolitan area. Also, it is initially occupied by households in the upper half of the national income distribution, because lower income households cannot afford to live there.

As time passes, the housing units in this neighborhood become older and less stylish compared to newer units. Housing fashions change swiftly in the United States—probably faster than anywhere else in the world. For example, the average size of new conventional single-family homes rose over 60 percent in eighteen years—from slightly under 1,000 square feet in 1950 to over 1,600 square feet in 1968.[2] Design changes like family rooms, built-in appliances, and bathroom counter-top sinks also hasten the obsolescence of older units. Eventually their increasing age generates higher maintenance costs, too.

At the same time, the real incomes of many households initially living in this neighborhood increase. Many move to even newer housing units that are larger, more stylish, and in "fancier" neighborhoods. Gradually the edge of settlement moves farther out, leaving this neighborhood surrounded by other urban developments. This makes it relatively more central but also more hemmed in and subject to higher traffic congestion. In addition, relatively lower income households continuously move into the housing in the area. They are larger and tend to use the housing more intensively. For most incoming households, this housing represents an improvement over the even older units from which they have moved.

As more time passes, the once new housing becomes less and less desirable compared to the newest and best in society, even if it is well maintained. Because it is occupied by a succession of *relatively* lower and lower income groups, it eventually houses groups with *absolutely* much lower incomes than those who first lived there. As long as the occupants have incomes high enough to maintain their properties, the neighborhood may remain in good physical condition. But in time, the annual costs of such maintenance become fairly high, while the occupants' annual incomes become quite low. Then the housing begins to deteriorate significantly. Households with alternative choices move elsewhere. Finally the housing becomes occupied by the lowest income groups in society and falls into extreme disrepair.

At that point, this housing has "trickled down" through

society's income distribution from near the top to the bottom. Its life cycle results in its becoming a "slum" in three to six decades after it was built. Along the way, it provided fine, or at least adequate, shelter for a succession of households. For most, it was an improvement over their past shelter as they moved upward through the housing inventory. But it has finally fallen to a quality level far below what society regards as "minimally acceptable."

Not all new neighborhoods undergo this life cycle. Some retain high relative desirability for decades, even centuries. They are usually located near some outstanding amenity, such as a lake, a major university, a park, or a downtown area. Certain Southern metropolitan areas also present an exception to this process. Because of racial segregation, local officials long ignored housing quality regulations in black-occupied areas, many of which were on the urban periphery or scattered in small pockets in more affluent neighborhoods. The preceding analysis is therefore more applicable in the Northeast, Midwest, and West than in the South. However, these non-Southern urban areas contain well over half of the nation's population.

The "trickling down" of urban neighborhoods has been accelerated by the absolute growth of low-income population in most metropolitan areas since World War II. This growth was stimulated by both massive in-migration and natural increase. After the postwar housing shortage began to diminish around 1950, poorer groups pushed outward from relatively deteriorated neighborhoods into better quality surrounding housing. The resulting transition from middle-income to low-income occupancy has occurred in thousands of urban neighborhoods across the country, moving them farther along in the "trickle-down" process.

This process neatly matches housing of various prices and quality levels with consumers at different income levels. Consequently, each household usually finds itself in an area occupied mainly by other households with incomes like its own and living in housing like its own in quality and price. Each neighborhood forms a relatively homogeneous rung on an

overall "economic ladder" that contains a tremendous variety
of different qualities (and prices) of housing and neighborhood
environments. So it offers a wide spectrum of housing choices
to individual households.

DIFFERENTIAL HOUSING LAW ENFORCEMENT

This combination of homogeneity within neighborhoods
and diversity among them is aided by differential enforcement
of laws concerning housing quality. In new-growth areas,
building and housing codes are rigorously enforced, preventing creation or maintenance of anything but relatively high
quality housing. True, prices for new units range anywhere
from $14,000 to $100,000 or more. But even $14,000 units are
of *relatively* high quality compared to the entire range of
construction possibilities. Their low costs result mainly from
smaller size, smaller lots, and less desirable locations than
costlier housing.

In somewhat older neighborhoods, housing codes are less
rigorously enforced because the units are both more deteriorated and more obsolete. Nevertheless, really poor maintenance is prohibited by moderately active code enforcement.

But in very low-income areas, where many households live
in extremely deteriorated units that clearly violate the law,
housing codes are almost totally unenforced. This is not a
conspiracy between evil landlords and local authorities.
Rather it is an economic necessity resulting mainly from the
poverty of the residents. They cannot afford enough rent to
allow property owners to maintain their housing at legal
quality levels and still obtain a reasonable return on their
investment. This result of the occupants' poverty is sometimes
aggravated by the destructive behavior of a minority of the
poor. Such behavior further increases the cost of maintaining
their housing at the legally required standards.

Under these circumstances, rigorous enforcement of housing
codes would require local authorities to evict thousands of
households from illegally substandard units. But where would
they go? There are nowhere near enough vacant units that
simultaneously meet all legally required quality standards and

have rents low enough so that the displaced households could afford them. These households would have to leave the area or live in the streets, as in Calcutta. To avoid these traumatic outcomes, authorities in every large American city largely ignore housing codes in older low-income neighborhoods.

Another adverse effect of rigorous code enforcement would be abandonment of housing by many owners. Bringing their buildings into legal conformity would require major investments. To produce adequate returns, owners would have to raise rents far beyond the ability of existing residents to pay. But people who could afford such rents will not move into neighborhoods occupied mainly by the very poor. As a result, owners who brought their properties into compliance could not recoup their investments. Rather than thus throw money away, many owners stop paying taxes, collect as much rent as possible with minimal maintenance, and eventually let the municipal government claim their properties for tax delinquency. Such abandonment has been occurring on an increasing scale in cities like New York, Detroit, and Saint Louis.

Public officials must ignore the law in many older low-income areas, or enforce it badly, because that law "requires" everyone to live in a quality of housing that thousands of poor households cannot afford. True, even the poor could enjoy "decent" housing if more affluent citizens would help them pay for it. But the resulting subsidy cost would be so enormous that American citizens are not willing to bear it. Yet we refuse to confront these realities by changing legal housing quality requirements to reflect more nearly what poor people can afford. Instead, we hypocritically "require" relatively high minimum quality standards for all households, since that does not "undemocratically discriminate" against the poor. Then we deliberately fail to enforce these standards so as to accommodate reality.

However, as noted above, our failure to enforce housing quality standards is not the same everywhere in metropolitan areas. These standards are rigorously enforced in *all* new-growth areas, thereby excluding almost all poor households.

Yet the same standards are ignored in older, deteriorated neighborhoods, thereby allowing poor households to remain. True, in most of the world, governments recognize the need for different housing quality standards for different income groups. But low quality housing is allowed *both* around the urban periphery where new growth is occurring and in older, deteriorated areas. This means that the very rich, the very poor, and other income groups all live relatively close together on the urban periphery and in the urban core.

In the United States, the "trickle-down" system minimizes such proximity. The only relatively low quality new housing units allowed in America are mobile homes, which are almost universally segregated from other new housing and forced to occupy the least desirable residential sites. Nevertheless, the demand for new low quality housing is so great that mobile home sales shot up to over 20 percent of all new housing starts in 1969, 1970, and 1971.

How the Trickle-Down Process Serves the Majority Well

The trickle-down process is relatively efficient economically. Every household occupies the type of housing it can best afford and is surrounded by neighbors at roughly the same economic level. But how about the social and psychological results? What quality of life does this process produce?

For the wealthiest households, this system is great. It allows them to live in high quality neighborhoods without any of the problems caused by poor residents. Local government doubly benefits from the absence of poor residents: it has a high per capita tax base because of high cost homes and low expenditure needs for assisting the unfortunate. Hence it can generate high per student spending on schools and still have low tax rates. Crime rates are low and most people do not fear walking the streets at any time.

For millions of American "middle-income" households (say, those with annual incomes from about $8,000 to $15,000 in 1969), the trickle-down system is also beneficial. They can find areas where others like themselves predominate and where there are few problems caused by poverty. Perhaps the houses are a bit older than in the most affluent neighborhoods, but the general quality of life is excellent compared to that prevalent in the best neighborhoods fifty years ago, in many other American neighborhoods today, or in most of the world throughout history. In 1969, 60.4 percent of all families in the United States had annual incomes of $8,000 or more. Within metropolitan areas, 66.2 percent had such incomes.[3]

In my opinion, the vast majority of these families are well served by the trickle-down process, though they do not fully understand it. They prefer living in neighborhoods occupied by others with incomes and housing quality about like their own. And they like not having really poor residents around. Therefore, the trickle-down process is probably successful in providing a majority of families in American metropolitan areas with "a decent home in a suitable living environment."

WHY THE TRICKLE-DOWN PROCESS IS DISASTROUS TO MILLIONS

For millions of the poorest households in American metropolitan areas, the trickle-down process is a disaster. It compels households with the lowest incomes and often the least competence to live concentrated together in our worst urban housing. This concentration has a "critical mass" effect that multiplies the negative impacts of poverty, creating entire neighborhood environments dominated by the conditions of poverty. These include certain problems and pathologies most intensively associated with indigence (although found among all income groups to some degree). The results are "crisis ghettos" marked by high rates of crime, vandalism, broken families, mental illness, delinquency, and drug addiction. These areas also have the lowest quality public schools, public services, and housing in urban society. Such neighborhoods are found mainly in central cities and some close-in suburbs because they contain the oldest remaining housing. The poorest people cluster there because these areas offer the lowest available occupancy costs.

Although crisis ghettos are small relative to the nation's

total population, they are absolutely huge in some cities. For example, in Cook County, Illinois (which contains Chicago), there were 512,000 people on welfare in April 1971. Over 100,000 lived in households composed of only one adult and six or more children.[4] It is hard for one adult to control six or more children effectively under the best of circumstances. Under extreme poverty in a deteriorated neighborhood, a sizable fraction of such households are very likely to exhibit some of the destructive behavior patterns described above.

Moreover, compelling thousands of such households to become concentrated in the worst urban housing causes a reverberation of their problems, greatly magnifying the total negative effects. Yet such concentration is inescapable as long as we administer housing quality laws so as to exclude the poor from most upper- and middle-income areas. Hence, it results from a combination of both poverty and exclusionary behavior.

Furthermore, the municipalities containing these concentrations are forced to try individually to cope with the worst social problems caused by urban society as a whole. Poor households generate unusually high public service costs while providing relatively low taxable resources. So local governments in many central cities and in some older suburbs must try to combat poor quality schools, high crime rates, high welfare support costs, and high fire incidence rates. Yet their assessed value bases are stagnant or declining (except for a few new downtown office buildings).

Understandably, these communities have a hard time attracting new high- or middle-income housing. Most people who can afford such housing do not want to live near poverty-laden areas or send their children to schools dominated by poor children. Thus spatial concentration of the worst urban poverty at the bottom of the trickle-down process is a central cause of many key economic and social difficulties in our large cities.

Viewed as a whole, the trickle-down process is an ingenious arrangement through which the major social costs of creating wonderful neighborhood environments for the wealthy and ·

good ones for the middle class are loaded onto the poorest households least capable of bearing such burdens. This process magnifies the burdens that poverty would generate if poor people were spread out in more neighborhoods. Many undesirable conditions in crisis ghettos are caused by the behavior of some of the poor themselves. Yet the majority of poor residents there do not engage in such behavior—they are just as appalled by it as the more affluent people who have fled elsewhere. In fact, innocent low-income residents of crisis ghettos are the principal victims of destructive behavior there. But they cannot join the wealthier families who have fled this environment, because those wealthier households have erected legal barriers to keep millions of decent but poor households from sharing in the higher quality environments they enjoy.

Most of the middle- and upper-income households so well served by the trickle-down process are not aware of the cruel costs it imposes upon the poor at the bottom of the heap. These more affluent citizens live spatially isolated from crisis ghettos, and their separation allows many to indulge in the morally complacent—and false—practice of blaming crisis ghetto conditions solely upon the residents. This self-righteous attitude ignores their own role in creating and sustaining those conditions by deliberately excluding all poor people from areas where they themselves live.

In my opinion, any arrangement that benefits the wealthy and the middle class at the expense of loading large costs onto the very poor is a gross injustice that cries out for correction. Yet that is precisely the effect of the entire trickle-down process that dominates urban development in the United States. And this situation is not a "natural" result of "free market forces." On the contrary, it is created, sustained, and furthered by public policies and laws that prevent free markets from operating. Those policies and laws are designed to protect the vested interests of the urban majority at a terrible cost to the poor, who constitute a relative minority in our society.

This book proposes a general strategy and specific tactics for changing the trickle-down process so as to ready its present unfair operation. I certainly do not advocate abandoning this process altogether. It serves the interests of most American households very well, and there is no other way to do so nearly as effectively. Besides, there is nothing wrong, in principle, with enabling most American households of *all* income groups—even the wealthiest—to live in housing that is not brand-new or that has been previously occupied by someone else. This must continue to happen, because our annual output of new housing units is so small (it has exceeded 2 million units only twice up through 1972) compared to our huge inventory of "used" housing (around 70 million units in 1972). Yet we need to make major changes in the way the trickle-down process works, so that it does not "automatically" create excessively large concentrations of the poorest urban households in the worst quality housing and neighborhoods.[5]

Undoubtedly, the urban majority that benefits by the trickle-down process will initially resist the main changes in that process proposed in this book. Getting those changes adopted will thus be politically difficult. It seems especially unlikely in the domestic political climate prevailing when this book was completed (early 1973). Yet one way to hasten the adoption of the required changes is to show how the fundamental injustice of American urban development can be remedied while still protecting the legitimate interests of the urban majority. That is what this book seeks to do.

2 Economic and Racial Differences between Central Cities and Suburbs

Do central cities really differ from suburbs? If so, how—and by how much? An accurate perspective on this subject requires recognizing three conditions: the great variety among individual suburbs, the growing similarity of suburban areas and central cities, and the remaining significant differences between them.

Individual suburbs vary tremendously. Some differ much more from others than suburbs as a whole differ from central cities as a whole. Many of the generalizations in this book must be qualified by this observation.

Furthermore, as suburbs have grown, they have acquired new facilities that make them far more comparable to central cities than they were twenty years ago. Some suburbs now contain giant shopping centers ringed with high-rise office buildings that rival older central business districts. In many metropolitan areas, suburbs now contain hospital complexes, colleges and universities, clusters of huge motels, legitimate theaters, fine restaurants, and even sports stadiums. They have also begun to exhibit many negative features of big cities, such as continual traffic congestion, smog, rising crime rates, and deteriorating older housing.

These similarities preclude glib generalizations that sharply contrast all suburbs with all central cities. Much more significant for public policy are the distinctions that can be made between relatively *new* portions of suburbs and central cities and *older* portions of both. The new portions are where new urban growth is now concentrated, or soon will be. The older portions are where urban decay is appearing, or soon could be.

If all relevant 1970 census data had been available when this book was written, these distinctions could have been more fully documented. Nevertheless, the suburban/central-city differences described here do offer approximate comparisons of *new-growth areas* (mostly but not always in suburbs) and *older potentially decaying areas* (mostly in central cities, but more and more frequently in older suburbs too).

Most of the key differences between central cities and suburbs are well known and have been extensively studied and documented. In order to avoid overwhelming readers with statistics, I have briefly summarized below the major differences relevant to this study without including detailed supporting data. The appendix presents such data in graphic form.[1]

The most important differences between central cities as a whole and suburbs as a whole are as follows:

1. In general, central cities contain higher proportions of low- and moderate-income households—especially poor ones—than suburbs, and lower proportions of upper-income households. However, a significant number of poor persons already live in suburban areas.

2. Suburban areas experienced much more total construction of new housing than central cities during the past decade. Yet suburban areas also experienced *less* new construction in relation to either population growth or housing inventory growth than either central cities or nonmetropolitan areas. Hence housing markets were moving farther away from "shortage" conditions in central cities than in suburbs during the 1960s.

3. The proportion of home ownership is greater among suburban residents than among central-city residents for both whites and blacks.

4. Suburban housing is generally more expensive than central-city housing for both owner-occupants and renters.

5. A much higher fraction of all neighborhoods experience nearly complete residential transition from one income or ethnic group to another in central cities than in suburbs in any given time period. This results from the steady expansion of both minority groups and relatively low-income groups within central cities. Also, population turnover tends to be higher in

very low-income neighborhoods than in other areas, and central cities contain more of the former than do suburbs. For these reasons many central-city neighborhoods and housing markets have been in a state of frequent or continuous ferment for much of the past twenty-five years. This instability is an important qualitative difference between life in these central-city neighborhoods and in most suburban neighborhoods.

6. The number and percentage of nonwhite residents—especially blacks—is much higher in central cities than in suburbs, on the average. The vast majority of suburbs are still overwhelmingly white in ethnic composition, as are most parts of most central cities. Yet many central cities—especially the larger ones—have sizable minority-group populations residing mainly in spatially segregated areas.

7. Population densities tend to be higher in central cities than in suburbs. But density falls in general with distance from the central business district; so some parts of central cities far from downtown have low densities, and some close-in suburbs have high densities.

8. Central cities on the average contain slightly higher percentages of older persons than do suburbs and somewhat lower percentages of households with school-age children. Hence, the median age in central cities is about two years higher than that in suburbs.

9. Suburban governments tend to spend a higher proportion of their total budgets for education and lower proportions for various social services than do central-city governments (considering all governmental agencies in each). Moreover, central-city governments generally provide a wider variety of public services and activities than suburban governments, and consequently they spend more per resident than suburban governments (though this does not necessarily mean that they have higher property taxes). To a great extent, these differences are related to varying city size—but central cities are usually much larger than individual suburbs.

10. Crime rates (for major crimes) are generally higher in large cities than in smaller ones, so central cities tend to have

significantly higher crime rates than suburbs. Although suburban crime rates have been rising more rapidly in recent years
than those in central cities, there is still a significant differential favoring the suburbs in most metropolitan areas.

3 The Growing Dominance of the Suburbs

The importance of opening up the suburbs depends greatly upon where the nation's future population and economic growth will be. The more such growth occurs in the suburbs, the more urgent will be the need to provide greater equality of access to the many benefits associated with it.

RECENT POPULATION GROWTH

In 1970 about 76.3 million Americans—37.6 percent of the nation—were suburbanites. That means they lived in the outlying portions of the 230 regions designated as "Standard Metropolitan Statistical Areas" by the Census Bureau. This was a larger number than lived in either the central cities of those same metropolitan areas (63.8 million, or 31.4 percent) or outside of metropolitan areas (63.0 million or 31.0 percent).[1]

The slight suburban preponderance in absolute population is not nearly as significant as the overwhelming suburban dominance of recent population growth in the United States. The suburban share of American population growth has risen steadily from 1900 to 1970, as indicated in table 1 and its accompanying figure. In contrast, the central-city share has been declining steadily since 1920, except for a moderate resurgence from 1940 to 1950 caused by wartime conditions. For the past two decades (from 1950 onward), suburban areas have "captured" around two-thirds of all population growth in the nation (64.3 percent in the 1950s and 70.5 percent in the 1960s).[2]

RECENT ECONOMIC GROWTH

Suburban dominance of American population growth has been accompanied by almost equal dominance of the economic expansion associated with population growth when the

Table 1
Percentage Shares of Total U.S. Population
Growth by Geographic Areas, 1900–70

Decade	All Met-ropolitan Areas	All Central Cities	All Suburbs	All Non-metropolitan Areas
1900–10	63.7	45.9	17.8	36.3
1910–20	76.4	54.7	21.7	23.6
1920–30	83.2	49.4	33.8	16.8
1930–40	65.9	27.0	38.9	34.1
1940–50	86.1	35.0	51.1	13.9
1950–60	84.4	20.1	64.3	15.6
1960–70	83.9	13.4	70.5	16.1

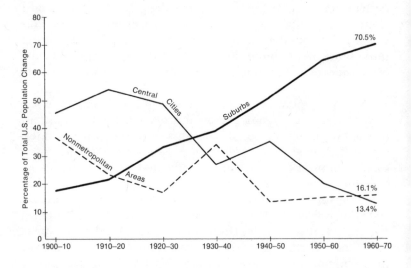

NOTE: Data derived from table A.1 in Appendix; source same as for that table.

Data for 1960–70 based on figures for 230 areas classified as metropolitan in 1970; all other decades based on figures for 212 areas classified as metropolitan in 1960.

added population is relatively affluent. Consequently, the vast majority of new homes, new apartments, new shopping centers, new schools, new streets, new parks, new roads, new highways, new public buildings, new factories, new sewer and water systems, and other new structures built in the United States in the past thirty years have been in the suburbs.

For the same reasons, *a preponderant majority of the net new jobs created in the United States recently have been located in the nation's suburbs.* It is true that many suburban residents commute to central-city jobs. It is also true that many new industrial plants have been located outside metropolitan areas. Nevertheless, almost all recent studies of employment location indicate that:

1. Suburban commuting to central cities is declining as a proportion of all work trips. In the nation's fifteen largest metropolitan areas, the fraction of all workers residing in the suburbs who also work there increased from 68 percent in 1960 to 72 percent in 1970. By now, only about one-fourth of all suburban-dwelling workers in these areas commute to central city jobs.[3]

2. Suburbs have almost totally dominated metropolitan-area employment growth in the recent past, while many older central cities have suffered serious economic declines. These conclusions are illustrated by data for the nation's fifteen largest metropolitan areas shown in table 2. Changes in employment from 1960 to 1970 by place of job for parts of each area are shown in both absolute numbers and percentages. These fifteen areas contained over 27 percent of all civilian employment in both 1960 and 1970. During the 1960s the total number of persons employed in the central cities of these areas combined declined by 836,000 (or 6.9 percent). In contrast, the total number employed in the suburbs rose by 3,086,000 (or 43.6 percent). Thus the suburbs in these fifteen areas captured 137 percent of all the net new jobs created there (more than 100 percent because central cities lost jobs). Nine of the fifteen central cities lost employment in this decade—six experiencing drops of more than 10 percent. Detroit lost more than one-fifth of its jobs in this period. In

Table 2
Civilian Employment Changes by Zone in the Fifteen
Largest Metropolitan Areas, 1960–70

Metropolitan Area	Total Employment Change		Central-City Employment Change	
	Number	Percentage	Number	Percentage
1. New York	14,000	0.3	−339,000	−9.7
2. Los Angeles–Long Beach	51,000	2.1	−137,000	−10.8
3. Chicago–Gary	277,000	11.3	−232,000	−13.9
4. Philadelphia	216,000	15.6	−98,000	−11.3
5. Detroit	170,000	13.9	−156,000	−22.5
6. San Francisco–Oakland	105,000	10.4	2,000	0.4
7. Washington, D.C.	332,000	43.9	9,000	1.9
8. Boston	68,000	7.4	−35,000	−8.6
9. Pittsburgh	24,000	3.2	12,000	4.4
10. Saint Louis	148,000	22.4	−61,000	−15.2
11. Baltimore	132,000	22.3	−22,000	−5.6
12. Cleveland	80,000	12.4	−71,000	−15.3
13. Houston	287,000	67.2	177,000	49.2
14. Minneapolis–Saint Paul	160,000	30.0	1,000	0.3
15. Dallas	186,000	46.4	114,000	37.6
Total	2,250,000	11.8	−836,000	−6.9

SOURCE: *New York Times* analysis of U.S. Census Bureau data, October 15, 1972, pp. 1, 58.

contrast, all fifteen suburban areas gained employment—ten experiencing increases of more than 60 percent, including three in which suburban jobs more than doubled in the decade. The suburban share of total employment rose in fourteen of the fifteen areas and exceeded 50 percent of all jobs in eight areas by 1970. By 1973 the suburbs in all fifteen areas

Table 2 (continued)

Suburban Employment Change		Percentage of Total Employment in Suburbs		
Number	Percentage	1960	1970	Change, 1960–70
353,000	24.9	28.8	35.9	7.1
188,000	16.2	47.8	54.3	6.5
509,000	64.4	32.2	47.5	15.3
314,000	61.5	37.0	51.8	14.8
326,000	61.5	43.3	61.4	18.1
103,000	22.7	44.9	50.0	5.1
323,000	117.9	36.2	54.9	18.7
103,000	20.2	55.5	62.2	6.7
12,000	2.5	64.0	63.7	−6.3
209,000	80.4	39.3	58.0	18.7
154,000	76.6	34.1	49.9	15.8
151,000	82.5	28.3	46.0	17.7
110,000	164.2	15.7	24.4	8.7
159,000	126.2	23.6	41.1	17.5
72,000	73.5	24.4	29.0	4.6
3,086,000	43.6	37.0	47.6	10.6

combined will contain more employment than the combined central cities.

3. Industrial and warehousing establishments have moved to lower density suburban locations in massive numbers since World War II—both by creating new facilities and by relocating older ones there.

4. The majority of new shopping centers have been built in the suburbs.

5. Only in three basic categories of employment are most large central cities holding their own in relative shares within each metropolitan area. These are office work, service jobs, and government jobs—including all levels of education.

Thus *the evidence is overwhelming that suburbs have been by far the most economically dynamic parts of the nation during the past twenty years or more.* This is true in terms of new public and private capital investment and new employment opportunities. In short, regarding economic growth, the suburbs are where the action is.

The Prospects for Future Suburban Dominance

Could a future decline in the attractiveness of suburbs drive many households back to central cities? Suburbs as a whole are becoming older, more congested, higher in density, more polluted, and plagued by higher crime rates and poorer schools. In short, many suburbs are coming to resemble central cities in everything except centrality.

Nevertheless, four factors strongly suggest that this decline in the "suburban-ness" of many suburbs—especially older ones—will not massively shift new residential construction to central cities. Suburban peripheral land is still much cheaper than almost any central-city land. Also, there is vastly more vacant land available in the suburbs than in central cities. Third, the largest central cities and many older suburbs will continue to experience spatial expansion of low-income groups already living there. Unless much of the future growth and spatial expansion of these groups is shifted to the suburbs, they will exert constant pressure to expand their share of the central cities' housing inventory. Hence even if central cities succeed in attracting potential suburbanites into new housing in some neighborhoods, they will lose far more of the same type of household in other neighborhoods because of continued expansion of their low-income populations. Thus, in spite of the highly visible construction of many new high-rise apartments in Chicago, Philadelphia, Boston, Saint Louis, and

Detroit, all of these cities experienced large population declines from 1960 to 1970.

Finally, central cities will not regain former growth rates because most are experiencing a long-range decline in population density. This shift is related to the dominance of urban transportation by automobiles and trucks. It has led to expansive, low-density settlement patterns—which have dominated suburban growth since World War II and even earlier. This means that the downtown business district is no longer the economically dominant hub of each metropolitan area. It is just one major node among several, and it competes with many outlying regional shopping–office–recreation centers. As a result, population densities in many older central cities have been declining for decades. Manhattan reached its peak density of 103,000 persons per square mile in 1910—dropping to 67,000 in 1970. Boston and Buffalo had their highest densities in 1930.

In fact, some observers argue that central cities are losing their basic economic functions.[4] Plagued by obsolete structures, high crime rates, congestion, vandalism, and concentrated poverty, they are unable to compete with suburbs as viable locations of economic activity. The resulting flight of employment to the suburbs removes the basic source of private income flows from many central-city neighborhoods. For all of the above reasons, I do not believe that central cities will "recapture" enough population and other growth to prevent continued suburban domination of future expansion.

Will the nonmetropolitan share of total growth rise enough to reduce future suburban dominance of growth significantly? I believe the nonmetropolitan share might rise in the near future, at least to some extent. However, if the central-city share remains at 15 percent or below, the nonmetropolitan share would have to rise above 25 percent in order to cut the suburban share below 60 percent. Yet the nonmetropolitan share has been 25 percent or more only once since 1910—during the Great Depression. It seems unlikely that this will occur again in the near future.

Furthermore, the Census Bureau's method of defining

metropolitan areas contains an inherent bias that tends to reduce nonmetropolitan growth. As soon as a particular nonmetropolitan city reaches a population of 40,000, and a total of 50,000 with its surrounding urbanized area, it is classified as a metropolitan area. In the 1970 census, eighteen such areas containing a 1960 population of nearly seven million were shifted from the nonmetropolitan to the metropolitan-area category.

LIKELY FUTURE SUBURBAN POPULATION GROWTH

It is reasonable to conclude that at least 60 to 70 percent of the American population growth in the next two to three decades will take place in the suburbs. This includes growth in places not yet counted as metropolitan areas that will be shifted into that category as they grow larger.

How great will this growth be? Table 3 presents three different assumptions about the future suburban share of total United States population growth: 65 percent, 70 percent, and 75 percent. The second is about equal to the actual share from 1960 to 1970, the first is somewhat more conservative, and the last is more expansive.

The lowest of these estimates yields a total suburban population growth of 15.0 million from 1970 to 1980, 15.2 million from 1980 to 1990, and 12.9 million from 1990 to 2000. This is an overall gain of 43.1 million from 1970 to 2000, or about 56 percent of the 1970 base.

The highest estimate indicates suburban population growth of 17.3 million from 1970 to 1980, 17.6 million from 1980 to 1990, and 14.9 million from 1990 to 2000. This is a total gain of 49.8 million from 1970 to 2000, or 65.3 percent of the 1970 base.

These estimates indicate that American suburbs will increase in population from 1970 to 2000 by about the same amount, or slightly more, than they grew in the first twenty-five years after World War II. That was the era of greatest suburban population expansion in American history up to now. As a result, by 1980, about 40 percent of the nation's total population will live in suburbs. By 2000, between 44 and

Table 3

Estimated Future Suburban Population Growth, 1970–2000
(In millions of persons)

Year	Total U.S. Population (Series E)[a]	Gain from Preceding Date	Suburban Growth	Total Suburban Population	Suburbs as % of U.S.
		65% Suburban Share			
1970	204.8	—	—	76.3[b]	37.6%
1980	227.8	23.0	15.0	91.3	40.1%
1990	251.2[c]	23.4	15.2	106.5	42.4%
2000	271.1	19.9	12.9	119.4	44.0%
		70% Suburban Share			
1970	204.8	—	—	76.3[b]	37.6%
1980	227.8	23.0	16.1	92.4	40.6%
1990	251.2[c]	23.4	16.4	108.8	43.3%
2000	271.1	19.9	13.9	122.7	45.3%
		75% Suburban Share			
1970	204.8	—	—	76.3[b]	37.6%
1980	227.8	23.0	17.3	93.6	41.1%
1990	251.2[c]	23.4	17.6	111.2	44.3%
2000	271.1	19.9	14.9	126.1	46.5%

[a] Based upon Series E projections in *Current Population Reports*, ser. P-25, no. 470, November 1971.
[b] Excludes Alaska and Hawaii—hence not perfectly comparable with 1970 total United States figure.
[c] Extrapolated from 1980 and 2000 projections and earlier 1990 projection.

46.5 percent will be suburban—as compared to 37.6 percent in 1970.

Clearly, suburban growth will be a major dynamic force in the nation's economy during the decades ahead.

4   The Benefits of Opening Up the Suburbs

Opening up the suburbs would produce the following seven major benefits:

1. Better access to expanding suburban job opportunities for workers in low- and moderate-income households —especially the unemployed
2. Greater opportunities for such households to upgrade themselves by moving into middle-income neighborhoods, thereby escaping from crisis ghetto conditions
3. Higher quality public schooling for children from low-income households who could attend schools dominated by children from middle-income households
4. Greater opportunity for the nation to reach its officially adopted goals for producing improved housing for low- and moderate-income households
5. Fairer geographic distribution of the fiscal and social costs of dealing with metropolitan-area poverty
6. Less possibility of major conflicts in the future caused by confrontations between two spatially separate and unequal societies in metropolitan areas
7. Greater possibilities of improving adverse conditions in crisis ghetto areas without displacing urban decay to adjacent neighborhoods

Each benefit consists of a likely outcome that would be superior to the probable results of continuing urban development along its present lines.

ACCESS TO JOB OPPORTUNITIES

Within metropolitan areas, unemployment is spatially concentrated in low-income central-city neighborhoods,[1] whereas job opportunities are growing fastest in the suburbs. Therefore, more effective linkages should be established between these two areas. In theory, there are three ways to do this: (1) locate more new jobs near poor central-city neighborhoods, (2) provide better transportation for central-city workers to reach suburban jobs, and (3) provide suburban housing opportunities for low-income households. In reality, the first two are not likely to occur on a big enough scale to cope with this problem. Moreover, the larger the future growth of suburban employment and the farther the edge of new suburban development from poor central-city areas, the more inadequate these two possibilities will become. Hence the best short-run solution, and the only feasible long-run solution, is to make more suburban housing available to relatively low-income households.

Suburban dominance of recent and future employment growth was discussed in chapter 3. If more than 80 percent of metropolitan-area population growth continues to occur in the suburbs, these areas will become more dominant regarding both new jobs and those arising from turnover in the existing work force. (Turnover is roughly proportional to total employment, rather than to growth in employment.) In addition, since suburban employers will have an even larger need for relatively low-paid workers, linking lower income workers with suburban jobs will become more and more important.

This linkage cannot be accomplished by diverting large numbers of new jobs from the suburbs to central-city, low-income areas. A few attempts have been made to create "ghetto industries," with mixed success, as in the Watts area of Los Angeles. Even a ten-fold increase in past successes would provide an insignificant number of new jobs for low-income workers as compared to the number that will arise in the suburbs.

How about improving transportation facilities linking low-income areas in central cities with suburban job centers? Most low-income workers and job seekers in poor central-city areas rely on public transportation. This is also true of most second job holders (often women) in moderate-income families. But nearly all existing public transportation networks are poorly structured to move people from central-city residential areas to suburban job centers during rush hours. More crucially, the basic low-density structure of suburban development means that most of the workers employed in suburban areas will have to use automobiles for commuting, either singly or in car pools. Yet many poor central-city workers cannot afford automobiles. Even if they could, the distances between poor central-city neighborhoods and many outlying suburban job locations are so great that commuting times would be well over one hour each way. So improving transportation between low-income central-city areas and suburban jobs—though desirable —is not the answer.

In the long run, the only way to establish the required linkages is to provide suburban housing opportunities for low- and moderate-income households near new job openings. However, even widespread dispersal of low- and moderate-income households within the suburbs will not solve the problem of transporting their members to work at scattered suburban job sites. Public transportation is far less extensive in suburban areas than in central cities, and under present arrangements, low-income workers living in suburbs would have almost as much trouble getting to nearby jobs as they do now from their central-city homes. But drastically reducing the basic commuting distance would surely simplify the problem, making it possible to find solutions with less public investment. Doing so is vital to the long-run process of maximizing the nation's economic output and reducing its social costs—including the costs of supporting the unemployed.

Escape from the Slums

Escaping from poverty through "upgrading" one's household is a long-established American tradition. It presumes that many low-income households can somehow generate the initiative and the money needed to move into a "better" neighborhood. Almost all Americans recognize the desirability of this process. Either they went through it themselves, or their parents or grandparents did. Yet such upgrading is impossible unless some relatively low-income households can move into predominantly middle-income areas.

This process does not necessarily imply that the lowest income households can or should move directly into the highest income neighborhoods. Rather it implies a whole series of neighborhoods with varying economic levels forming a "socioeconomic ladder" that mobile families can climb. A family moving into any of these neighborhoods is usually trying to escape from a lower quality neighborhood by enjoying physically better housing and surroundings and by associating with higher income neighbors. If some households with relatively low incomes compared to the local average are denied entry at any level on the ladder, the entire process will stop working effectively.

At present, most of the higher rungs on this socioeconomic ladder—and many middle ones—are located in America's suburbs. Effective upward mobility requires that hundreds of suburban middle- and upper-income neighborhoods be open to households with incomes below the local average. The more obstacles created to such entry, the more difficult it will be for low- and moderate-income families all the way down the ladder to upgrade themselves.

Unfortunately, the traditional upgrading process actually prevents millions of Americans at the bottom of this ladder from escaping their relatively miserable neighborhoods. It does so by linking general quality of neighborhood with household income or wealth. Those who can afford to buy a good environment get one; those who cannot afford it must accept much worse environments. (For ethnic minorities, however, racial prejudice severely limits the upgrading possibilities that would be available if only ability to pay were considered.)

A great deal of evidence indicates that real improvement of the most deprived households in our society requires their leaving the areas where they now live—areas dominated by the damaging influences described in chapter 1. As long as the most deprived households live in such areas, their members do not have much chance to significantly improve themselves economically, socially, or culturally.

Such areas contain two different types of low-income households. Those whom I will call the *mainstream poor* consider themselves full-fledged members of our society who are in a relatively short-term state of economic deprivation. Some are still young and therefore have not yet attained the income levels they are striving for. Others have suffered some temporary disabilities or economic setbacks that they expect to overcome in the future. Still others are households of elderly people who formerly enjoyed better economic status but are now retired from economic activity. The mainstream poor are generally upwardly mobile and exhibit aspirations and behavior patterns identical with those of most middle-income groups. In contrast, the *left-out poor* have become convinced that they are not full-fledged members of our society. Their basic aspirations are also the same as those of most middle-income Americans, but they do not really believe they can achieve those aspirations. They have lost confidence in themselves because of repeated experiences of failure, which in turn stem from such causes as racial discrimination, lack of skills, difficulties in school, and chronic unemployment.

Some sociologists believe this group constitutes a separate "lower class" or "culture of poverty" and its members exhibit behavior patterns different from most middle-class Americans because of basically differing values.[2] But I subscribe to the theory that these non-middle-class behavior patterns represent adaptations to their "left-out" status and the many problems it generates rather than any fundamental divergence of values.[3] Certain key differences between these two types of low-income households will be discussed further in later chapters. At this point, it is sufficient to emphasize that both types are present in urban poverty concentrations, and both would benefit from leaving those concentrations.

As I pointed out in chapter 1, the concentration of both types of deprived households together in crisis ghetto environments is no accident. It is the inexorable result of both poverty and the trickle-down process that dominates urban development in the United States. Preventing concentrated poverty from debilitating these deprived areas would require either or both of two actions. One is a massive social effort to alter basic conditions there. At present, no such effort is being seriously considered by either major political party. Even if tried, it would not work if it left many of the least capable households clustered together without any significant number of more capable households present.

The second possible remedy is a movement of low-income households into areas where influences similar to those in middle-class neighborhoods are dominant. This would also be a necessary part of any massive program to improve conditions in the most deprived areas, as noted above. In all cases, *some residential mixing of deprived households with nondeprived households, with the latter exerting a dominant influence, is necessary to achieve a significant upgrading of the former.* This point is discussed in detail in chapter 9.

Some people may ask, "Why do we need special public policies to encourage such mixing when we never had them in the past? If 'spontaneous' upgrading is so difficult today, how did the large existing middle class ever rise out of its lower income origins?" In reality, considerable "spontaneous" upgrading of this type still occurs. Yet several key changes in conditions make it more difficult than earlier in this century— and almost impossible for many Americans. Up to around 1930, most American cities had relatively high density residential neighborhoods linked to nearby jobs by public transportation. Although high quality neighborhoods were quite distinct from poverty-ridden slums, average housing quality standards were much lower and not rigorously enforced by public agencies. Hence there was far closer spatial intermixture of both individual housing units and whole neighborhoods containing occupants with widely varying incomes. Moreover, the proportion of jobs available to low skilled workers was quite high, and those jobs were easily accessible to the poor by public transportation.

The recent shift to larger, lower density, automobile-dominated settlement patterns has greatly increased the separation of the poor from the non-poor residentially. It has also made it harder for low-income workers to reach the areas of fastest job growth. At the same time, the proportion of all jobs available to relatively low-skilled workers has dropped sharply. In contrast, housing quality standards—and the cost of meeting them—have risen sharply. These standards are now rigorously enforced by public agencies in many better quality areas. The incorporation of low-density settlements into legally separate jurisdictions with their own zoning rules and building codes has put more barriers between the poor and the non-poor.

Ethnic discrimination against more easily visible minority groups adds still another handicap making upward mobility more difficult for those at the bottom of the pile. For all of these reasons, without changes in existing policies, spontaneous upgrading will certainly not take place fast enough to offset the ill effects of concentrated poverty described in chapters 1 and 9.

IMPROVED EDUCATIONAL OPPORTUNITIES

Improving the education of low-income children is a key part of any long-range program to raise the nation's general educational levels, combat unemployment, increase productivity, reduce economic dependency, and make equality of opportunity more meaningful. Experience suggests that this objective would be more fully attained if many more low-income children attended classes dominated by children from middle-income households. Since a large fraction of the nation's middle-income households live in suburbs, opening up the suburbs to greater residence by low- and moderate-income households would significantly improve the educational achievement of their children.

Several studies show that educational achievement scores of many low-income children tend to improve somewhat when they attend classes in which middle-income children predominate. The largest such study—involving over 600,000 public school pupils—was conducted for the U.S. Office of Education by Professor James Coleman.[4] This study indicated that the family backgrounds of both black and white students were far more important influences on their verbal achievement scores than the nature or quality of the schools they attended. It also indicated that low-income students attending schools with predominantly middle-income or higher status student bodies tended to have higher verbal achievement scores than those attending predominantly low-income schools, although this relationship was much weaker than that related to the individual student's home background. Some of this report's findings have been challenged on complex methodological grounds.[5] Nevertheless, even its critics appear to agree it shows that the achievement scores of low-income students are more likely to be improved by shifting them from mainly low-income to mainly middle-income schools than by leaving them in their former schools and spending much more money per student there.

Furthermore, placing low-income children in schools attended mainly by middle-income children usually improves the quality of the educational inputs they receive. By "educational inputs," I mean quality of teachers, availability of books and teaching aids, physical adequacy and condition of buildings and facilities, availability of special counseling and guidance, and total expenditures per student. In most metropolitan areas, many of these inputs are of higher quality in the average suburban school than in the average central-city schools serving low-income neighborhoods. This is true partly because suburban schools spend more money per student per year on the average.

Many low-income children would benefit from attending suburban, mainly middle-income schools even if they did not make higher achievement test scores. Education has many objectives besides acceptable test scores. They include learning to function effectively in a democratic society, developing a strong sense of identity and adequate self-confidence, and preparing for adult occupational roles. Presumably, most of these objectives are well served by improving the quality of educational inputs. If this were not so, suburban parents would surely not tax themselves to purchase such inputs.

I do not wish to exaggerate the educational benefits of opening up the suburbs. The recent research findings of Christopher Jencks indicate that the upgrading effects of such socioeconomic integration in schools would not even come close to eliminating existing educational inequalities.[6] Jencks emphasizes that the impact of schools upon the cognitive capabilities of students is probably far less significant than the impacts of heredity, home conditions, peer group behavior, and perhaps even television. Yet it is hard to believe that students from poor families who now attend crisis ghetto schools would not receive a better quality of whatever it is that schools do for students if they attended suburban schools where most students were from middle-income households. Numerous descriptions of chaotic classroom conditions, shortages of books and supplies, high absenteeism among teachers, high fractions of psychologically disturbed students, violent behavior in halls and outside school buildings, and other negative conditions in crisis ghetto schools convince me that many potentially able students there are deprived of valuable opportunities for learning that they would receive in most suburban schools. This is generally believed to be the case by parents in both types of areas, too. In spite of Jencks's findings, I am convinced that opening up the suburbs would indeed improve the quality of education for hundreds of thousands of children from low- and moderate-income households.

If socioeconomic integration in classrooms and improved educational inputs would benefit low-income children, why not provide those advantages without moving their households to the suburbs? Such children could be bused to predominantly middle-income schools instead. Or special "enrichment" programs could raise per pupil expenditures in big-city, low-income schools.

Unfortunately, both of these suggestions have severe limitations. Busing could cause some socioeconomic (and racial) integration around the edges of large low-income neighborhoods in big cities. But in our largest cities, concentrations of low-income households (often black and Puerto Rican) are huge. Busing any large number of poor children to predominantly middle-income schools would require excessively long trips. Moreover, busing to achieve economic integration would be strongly opposed politically if it also involved racial integration, which it would in many areas. Finally, current sentiment concerning big-city school systems favors greater *decentralization* of authority rather than the greater centralization required for metropolitan-wide busing. So busing seems both unworkable and undesirable as the *sole* means of attacking this problem (though I believe it is still useful in many situations).

On the other hand, simply spending more money in schools attended mainly by children from poor households does not improve their education very significantly. This is a highly controversial subject, so no statements about it are final. Yet most so-called compensatory education projects have produced no measurable improvements in educational results. True, some important educational *inputs* have been upgraded. But many well-informed observers believe classrooms dominated by children from very low-income households cannot be much improved by spending more money. Others object because this conclusion seems to condemn so many big-city children to receiving a second-rate education. But they have yet to develop a proven method of counteracting these disadvantages, even when more money is available. My own belief is that money alone cannot overcome the disadvantages mentioned above. Given this fact, we should at least test the economic integration of a large number of low-income households with children in suburban areas. At the same time, we should also test other ways of improving education within big-city, low-income schools. It is too early to decide what one policy—if any—will prove worthy of the greatest support.

Adding children from low- and moderate-income homes to mainly middle- and upper-income suburban schools would greatly widen the spectrum of home backgrounds in those schools. This would broaden the experience and outlooks of the children themselves, who would *all* be better equipped to live harmoniously in a world of immensely different cultures and peoples. It might even stimulate suburban educators to adapt their curricula and methods of teaching to better inculcate a sense of respect for diversity in their students—and themselves. The result might be a significant improvement in the education received by all American children.

Achievement of National Housing Goals

In the Housing and Urban Development Act of 1968, Congress "reaffirmed" its 1949 national housing goal of "realization as soon as feasible . . . of a decent home and a suitable living environment for every American family." Congress further declared that "this national housing goal . . . can be substantially achieved within the next decade by the construction or rehabilitation of 26 million housing units, 6 million of these for low- and moderate-income families."

The United States is not likely to create an additional 26 million housing units before 1978.[7] It is far more feasible— though still unlikely—to create 6 million additional housing units for low- and moderate-income families in this decade, or an average of 600,000 per year. However, even achieving more modest targets concerning such housing would require con- structing many thousands of new units each year for such households on vacant suburban land. In short, it would necessitate opening up the suburbs.

Most of the worst housing remaining in the United States in 1970 was outside of metropolitan areas. In 1960—the last year for which the Census Bureau tabulated "substandard" housing units—64 percent of the 11.4 million such units were in nonmetropolitan areas, 21 percent in central cities, and 15 percent in suburbs.[8] Many of the substandard units located in central cities in 1960 have been demolished, though further deterioration has created others. My estimate is that about 75 percent of the worst quality housing remaining in the United States lies outside of metropolitan areas; 15 percent is in central cities; and 10 percent is in suburbs.

Should we replace these units with the same emphasis on nonmetropolitan areas? No, because people are still moving from nonmetropolitan to metropolitan areas. If we allocated the replacement units in proportion to likely *future growth,* then 65 to 75 percent would be built in metropolitan areas. If we divided these units in proportion to *total present population,* then 69 percent would be in metropolitan areas. I assume that 70 percent should be in metropolitan areas. If the "target" is 6.0 million such units by 1978 (as Congress has declared), that means creating 4.2 million new units for low- and moderate-income households in metropolitan areas between 1968 and 1978.

Could most of these units be built in central cities? Placing them there would greatly raise per unit costs. Vacant land is far more expensive in central cities, and they do not contain enough *usable* vacant land to absorb many more units. Occupied land would have to be bought and cleared—and that is even more expensive. The clearance and renewal process takes six to nine years to complete, so it requires immense administrative and waiting costs as compared to building on vacant land. And political resistance to relocation, clearance, and renewal in big cities has become intense.

Furthermore, accommodating most of the planned 4.2 million new metropolitan-area units for low- and moderate-income households within central cities would require an unrealistically enormous increase in construction of *all* housing in such cities. From 1960 to 1970, about 3.8 million new units were built in central cities, or 380,000 per year. But most were for middle- and upper-income households, because of the high cost of new central-city housing.

If all of the future target rate of 420,000 low- and moderate-income units per year were built in central cities, that would create a huge increase in the total number of units built there each year. Moreover, well over half of all new housing built in central cities would then be for low- and moderate-income households, which would speed up the transition of many central cities toward greater dominance by the poor and the near-poor. Most central-city governments would be appalled at such a prospect. In fact, they would like to *reverse* that transition by concentrating on the construction of new middle- and upper-income units to counteract the basic "trickling down" of their huge older housing stock toward lower-income groups. Most big-city governments would strongly resist any major shift of new construction toward dominance by housing for low- and moderate-income groups. Therefore it seems clear that a big share of the national target—perhaps half or more—would have to be created in suburbs.

Even if the planned time period for eliminating all housing deficiencies is extended to twenty years, the basic problem will remain the same: central cities alone cannot accommodate the new housing units for the poor and near-poor that are required to end the inadequacies of their housing in metropolitan areas.

REDISTRIBUTION OF THE COSTS OF COMBATING POVERTY

Concentration of poor metropolitan-area households within central cities imposes an unjust fiscal and social burden upon the residents and governments of those cities. Suburbanites receive a majority of the benefits of metropolitan living because they outnumber central-city residents and enjoy better neighborhood environments, on the average. But they escape paying even a proportionate share of the costs of those benefits.

The fiscal disparities between central-city and suburban governments were described by the Advisory Commission on Intergovernmental Relations in a 1967 report as follows:

> There is a growing concentration of the "high cost" citizen in the central city. There is every reason to believe this trend will continue. . . . For example, 27 percent of Maryland's population is located in Baltimore, yet 71 percent of Maryland's AFDC case load is to be found in that city.
>
> The large central cities are in the throes of a deepening fiscal crisis. On the one hand, they are confronted with the need to satisfy rapidly growing expenditure requirements triggered by the rising number of "high cost" citizens. On the other hand, their tax resources are growing at a decreasing rate (and in some cases actually declining), a reflection of the exodus of middle and high

income families and business firms from the central city to suburbia.

A clear disparity in tax burden is evident between central city and outside central city. Local taxes in the central cities average 7.6 percent of the personal income of their residents; outside the central cities they equal only 5.6 percent of income.

On the educational or "developmental" front, the central cities are falling farther behind their suburban neighbors with each passing year. In 1957 the per pupil expenditures in the 37 metropolitan areas favored the central city slightly—$312 to $303 for the suburban jurisdictions. By 1965, the suburban jurisdictions had forged far ahead—$574 to $449 for the central cities. . . . [Yet] the central city school districts must carry a disproportionately heavy share of the educational burden—the task of educating an increasing number of "high cost" underprivileged children. *Children who need education the most are receiving the least!*

On the municipal service or custodial front, the presence of "high cost" citizens, greater population density, and the need to service commuters force central cities to spend far more than most of their suburban neighbors for police and fire protection and sanitation services. The 37 largest central cities had a non-educational [municipal] outlay of $232 per capita in 1965— $100 greater than their suburban counterparts.[9]

These conclusions clearly show the unjust consequences of concentrating the metropolitan poor in central cities. After all, urban poverty is not *caused* by central cities. Rather, it results from the way our industrialized, urbanized society operates as a whole. Poor citizens become concentrated in central cities for two main reasons. First, most of the oldest, least expensive housing is located there, along with many of the low-skill jobs and social services on which poor households depend. Second, they are prevented from living elsewhere by laws that deliberately raise housing costs in order to protect the investments and environments of non-poor suburbanites.

In reality, the central city and every suburb in each metropolitan area are specialized parts of the same basic economy. They are integrally related to each other in the same way that a man's lungs and eyes are parts of his body. It is therefore absurd for any one part of the metropolitan area to declare itself "autonomous" or "separate" from the remainder and hence "not responsible" for bearing any of the costs of what happens in other specialized areas. Every supposedly "separate" community not only depends utterly upon other areas for some of its essential services; it has also helped to create the very problems it declares are none of its concern, as described in chapter 1. Yet many suburbanites insist that their communities should remain "completely independent" when making decisions about who shall live there. But those decisions directly affect people who do *not* live there, too, including the poor, by determining where they *can* live—without giving them any voice in the decision.

Admittedly, opening up the suburbs is not the only way to counteract existing fiscal disparities. One much simpler remedy would be dissolving the political boundaries that fragment each metropolitan area and creating a single metropolitan government. This has been done in Indianapolis, Nashville, and Jacksonville. But it has not been done in 227 other metropolitan areas. True, most voters in some of these areas might choose metropolitan government over opening up their own communities to more low- and moderate-income households if forced to make a clear-cut choice between these two alternatives. Yet I doubt that any such sharp dichotomous choice will emerge in most metropolitan areas. Rather, voters are likely to continue rejecting strong metropolitan governments in order to preserve certain local authorities and powers that they value highly. Another possible remedy would be massive federal subsidy programs aimed at upgrading central-city poverty areas and financed by federal income taxes. But it is now clear that Congress will not support such programs. As long as suburbanites regard poverty as "somebody else's worry," they are not likely to accept their own obligation to bear more of the fiscal, social, and personal costs of coping with it. Hence they will not support politically even the purely financial redistribution of burdens necessary to correct metropolitan fiscal disparities without relocating the poor. Only when they encounter poverty in their own neighborhoods will they be strongly motivated to take effective action against it.

The above argument will probably not appeal to most suburbanites. Few people are sympathetic to requests that they start becoming involved with problems they have been deliberately fleeing for years. Yet there is a crucial difference in scale and intensity between the poverty that suburbanites would encounter if they opened up their own communities as I am suggesting and the poverty in central cities from which they have often fled. In many central-city neighborhoods, poverty and deprivation are overwhelming because of their dominance of the local environment. But opening up a prosperous suburb to a relatively limited influx of low- and moderate-income households would produce an entirely different context for poverty. The middle- and upper-income character of the community would remain dominant. Relatively well-off suburbanites could become personally, governmentally, and fiscally involved in helping the poor without being overwhelmed by the immensity and intransigence of the poverty they faced. Thus, diluting urban poverty by spreading it over a much broader landscape might produce qualitatively different—and much less forbidding—problems than concentrating urban poverty in a few highly deprived areas. This possibility coincides with a spreading desire among relatively affluent citizens in our society, especially the young, to become personally more involved with basic problems.

Perhaps these thoughts are overly idealistic. They are based upon what has been called the "contact theory" of improving relationships among members of diverse groups. This theory states that initial hostility and suspicion of groups toward each other can be reduced and perhaps even eliminated if members of each group come in frequent personal contact with members of the other groups *within a fundamentally positive context.* That means the group members encounter each other in situations that are "naturally" friendly, cooperative, and mutually beneficial, rather than in situations of conflict or with antagonistic objectives. Frequent repetition of such positively oriented contacts will teach members of each group that members of the other groups are essentially like themselves and can be treated decently to the benefit of all. However, if intergroup contacts occur in a basically negative context, increasing the frequency of those contacts can aggravate the initial suspicions and hostilities.

I believe the possibility of positively oriented contacts between the poor and the non-poor would be much greater if they frequently encountered each other in daily life in areas where poverty was not dominant. This situation would produce better results and create a greater possibility of social justice than either a total lack of daily contact between these groups or continuation of their contact in the process of "massive neighborhood transition" from non-poor to poor occupancy. Today there is an almost complete lack of contact between most suburbanites and most poor urban households. Contact at work and in the process of massive economic transition at the edge of low-income ghettos are the two basic forms of interaction between most lower-middle-income urban households and the urban poor. The bitterness and conflicts involved in neighborhood transition make that form of contact a strongly negative one. Opening up the suburbs would greatly increase the chances of changing these forms of intergroup contact to others occurring in a positive context. That in turn might improve the quality of justice in our society and the attitudes and behavior that more affluent people adopt toward the poor. These things are surely influenced by the manner in which the poor and non-poor encounter each other.

Avoiding a Divided Society

In 1968, the National Advisory Commission on Civil Disorders, considering the long-range consequences of continuing to concentrate our urban black population in central cities, wrote:

> The nation is rapidly moving toward two increasingly separate Americas. Within two decades, this division

could be so deep that it would be almost impossible to unite: a white society principally located in suburbs, in smaller central cities, and in the peripheral parts of large central cities, and a Negro society largely concentrated within large central cities. The Negro society will be permanently relegated to its current status, possibly even if we expend great amounts of money and effort in trying to "gild" the ghetto. In the long run, continuation and expansion of such a permanent division threatens us with two perils. The first is the danger of sustained violence in our cities. . . . The second is the danger of a conclusive repudiation of the traditional American ideals of individual dignity, freedom, and equality of opportunity.[10]

The commission rejected two spatially separate but unequal societies. Instead, it advocated *both* large-scale upgrading of ghetto areas within central cities *and* the movement of many black households to the suburbs. Its recommendations included creation of large amounts of housing for low- and moderate-income households outside central-city black neighborhoods.

Undoubtedly, the spatial separation of the poor from the non-poor in our metropolitan areas is nowhere near as striking as the spatial separation of blacks from whites, as indicated in chapter 2. Suburbs as a whole contained 5.4 million poor people in 1970—or 67 percent as many as the 8.2 million poor in central cities. In fact, 48 percent of all poor whites living in metropolitan areas in 1968 were suburbanites, as compared to 23 percent of all poor nonwhites.[11] Suburbs are wealthier on the average than central cities, and they are becoming more so. But there are millions of poor suburbanites, and many older suburbs are now experiencing the same concentration of low-income populations that has long troubled central cities. It seems that the nation is not in any real danger of developing a critical central-city/suburban split along purely economic lines, since urban poverty is found in both areas.

Yet continued exclusion of almost all low- and moderate-income households *from suburban new-growth areas* will produce undesirable divisiveness. For one thing, it will reduce opportunities for blacks to move to the suburbs. The black population is still much poorer than the white population on the average, and creating more suburban housing opportunities for low- and moderate-income groups would—in theory at least—improve suburban housing choices for a higher proportion of urban blacks than urban whites.

In reality, blacks will probably be much less aggressive about taking advantage of such new opportunities than whites. Not many blacks have moved to the suburbs up to now—even among those who could afford it. In fact, I am convinced that the belief of many whites that opening up the suburbs will cause an immediate, large-scale influx of black households is completely false. Under almost any circumstances imaginable, the vast majority of low- and moderate-income households who would move into new suburban housing would be white. Nevertheless, if even 10 percent were black, that would create at least some integration of black households throughout the suburbs—especially in many new-growth areas. Failure to create more such housing in suburbs would continue to confine black households mainly to central cities.

A second divisive impact of such failure will be severe spatial separation of the poor from the non-poor within suburbia itself. The rapidly expanding, economically dynamic new-growth suburbs on the edges of each metropolitan area will be populated almost entirely by middle- and upper-income households. In contrast, nearly all suburban low- and moderate-income households will be concentrated in older suburbs near the central city. Different economic groups will continue to attend and patronize completely separate schools, churches, shopping centers, and community activities. Yet I believe our society has much to gain by increasing daily contacts between income groups—if they occur in positive, nonhierarchical settings (not just at work, where the poor are subordinated to their more affluent superiors). I do not wish to exaggerate the potential fruitfulness of such contacts. The long historic self-separation of the private lives of the poor, the middle class, and the rich is not likely to disappear in our society—or any other—for a long time, if ever. Nevertheless, we need greater appreciation and acceptance among all Americans of the true value of diverse outlooks, life styles, economic levels, occupations, and cultural views. Opening up the new-growth areas of our suburbs to more low- and moderate-income housing could increase that appreciation significantly.

HALTING URBAN DECAY

Adverse conditions in big-city crisis ghettos cannot be improved without spreading urban decay to adjacent neighborhoods unless low- and moderate-income housing is dispersed to neighborhoods distant from these ghettos. This benefit is the subject of chapter 11, where it is discussed in detail.

5   The Costs and Who Should Pay Them

Nearly all new-growth suburbs and many older ones are closed to millions of American households because local laws force residents there to pay housing and other costs beyond the means of people with low and moderate incomes. The benefits of opening up the suburbs cannot be obtained unless these local laws are changed or public subsidies are used to help such households pay the required costs.

But why should other households be forced to pay for providing suburban amenities to those who cannot now afford them? Is it not more in the American tradition for each household to enjoy only those amenities it can pay for on its own? Many Americans—including President Nixon—have raised these questions. The answers set forth here will not satisfy everyone, but they should indicate that the issues involved are more complex and ambiguous than the rather simple view of social justice suggested by these questions.

HOUSING SUBSIDIES

The biggest cost of opening up the suburbs that cannot be borne by low- and moderate-income households themselves consists of the capital and operating costs of the housing they would occupy. In most cases, occupying "decent quality" suburban housing is so expensive that a low- or moderate-income household can do so only if it receives some type of housing subsidy.

A housing subsidy is any form of financial assistance that a government provides to help a household pay for its housing. In theory, a household "needs" any subsidy only when its income is so low that it suffers from "poverty" in regard to the aspect of life covered by that subsidy—whether it is food, housing, medical care, or some other basic requirement. "Poverty," in turn, means that the household experiences a "deficiency gap" between the fraction of its income that society believes it should "normally" devote to that particular aspect of life and the cost of enjoying the socially defined minimum standard of that commodity. The "normal share" of income that society has traditionally defined as appropriate for housing is about 25 percent (some more recent studies use 20 percent). Thus the size of the housing deficiency gap for a poor household is the amount by which 25 percent of its income (or 20 percent) falls short of paying the cost of occupying housing of a "minimally acceptable" size and quality for that size of household.

Several points about this definition should be emphasized. Anything that raises the income of a household with a deficiency gap reduces the size of the gap, if other things remain the same. All income support programs—such as the welfare program—are thus intimately related to housing subsidies. Also, anything that changes the quality level regarded as minimally acceptable influences the size of the deficiency gap for all households and the number of households with such gaps. The minimally acceptable quality level in America keeps rising as our economic system improves general living standards. Thus, the very success of our economy creates ever larger "needs" to subsidize those who have fallen behind economically. It also increases the per household cost of enabling them to "catch up" with "normal" households. Anything that changes the cost of producing a given level of housing quality—either up or down—also alters the size of the deficiency gap. In this way local laws that raise housing costs increase the size of the per household subsidy required to enable low- and moderate-income households to live there.

A final observation about housing subsidy gaps is that their major cause is poverty, not physically deficient housing. Most low-income urban households in America occupy decent quality housing units but pay relatively high fractions of their incomes to do so. They suffer from what I call *financial housing needs* rather than *physical housing needs*. The latter arise when households occupy physically inadequate dwelling units, whatever they pay for them, because there are not enough physically adequate units in the right locations to supply one for every household. The Urban Institute estimated that about 12.8 to 18.3 million American households suffered from financial housing needs in 1969—although most of those households lived in physically decent dwellings.[1] In contrast, probably somewhat less than half as many American households occupied physically inadequate dwellings in 1970, and most of these were in rural areas.

We can immediately conclude that some form of direct housing subsidy would be required to eliminate or even significantly reduce the housing deficiency gap now experienced by millions of American households. No one knows exactly how many households have such a gap, but the number is certainly larger than the total households considered "poor" by the official government definition, which is based on food requirements. As of 1970, about 25 million Americans—13 percent of the nation—were officially considered poor.

Realistically, the federal government will almost certainly not raise housing subsidies enough to close the total housing deficiency gap in the foreseeable future. The cost would be too great to receive congressional support. In other words, we do not really want to "solve" the nation's housing problem, insofar as doing so could be accomplished by housing subsidies. One indication of this is the persistent refusal of Congress to close the food deficiency gap in the United States. Yet that gap is much smaller in dollars than the housing deficiency gap, and good food is clearly more important to a decent life than good housing.[2]

THE PROBLEM OF HIGH HOUSING STANDARDS

If housing costs in suburban areas were much lower, then low- and moderate-income households could move there without large public subsidies. Why are these housing costs so high? Most analysts seeking to answer this question break down total housing occupancy costs into the costs of construction (land, labor, materials, and financing) and of operation (property taxes, insurance, and maintenance). Then they show how each of these components has been rising rapidly in recent years.

However, underlying these factors is a more fundamental cause of high housing costs that is often ignored or treated exclusively in analyses of zoning or density restrictions. This is the quality standards that newly built suburban (and other) housing units are required to meet. These standards involve minimum size requirements for the housing unit and various rooms in it; requirements for use of specific materials and construction methods; and minimum lot size and building spacing requirements (such as minimum set-backs of the house from the front, back, and sides of the lot). Whenever a locality's codes require minimum structure and lot sizes, they place an automatic floor under the cost of housing created there. The bigger the minimum requirement, the higher the costs of "legally built" housing.

In 1967 the National Commission on Urban Problems conducted a nationwide survey of governments issuing zoning or building codes.[3] It showed that for one-story single-family residences, among metropolitan municipalities containing 5,000 to 49,999 persons, 11.4 percent required such dwellings to contain 1,000 square feet or more, 17.7 percent required at least 800 to 999 square feet, and 12.3 percent required a minimum of 600 to 799 square feet.

Minimum lot size requirements are even more common— and more biased toward raising suburban housing costs. The commission's 1967 survey showed that 25 percent of the metropolitan-area municipalities containing 5,000 or more people permitted *no* single-family housing on lots less than one-half acre in size. In Connecticut in 1967, over half of all residentially zoned vacant land in the state was for lots of one- or two-acre minimum size. It was not easy to escape these requirements by building multifamily housing, either, because little suburban land was zoned for such housing. In the New York metropolitan area, for example, 99.2 percent of all undeveloped land zoned for residential construction required single-family dwellings.

Building codes are the third source of cost-increasing construction requirements. In 1967, 80 percent of the municipalities and townships with 5,000 or more persons had building codes. However, most had failed to update their codes to allow new cost-reducing construction methods. Among all local governments with building codes, 63 percent prohibited the use of plastic pipe in drainage systems; 42 percent prohibited off-site pre-assembled bathroom plumbing units; and 46 percent prohibited pre-assembled electrical harnesses. All of these are technically acceptable and safe practices that lower costs.

Thus, *legally required minimum standards for structure size, lot size, and building methods create relatively high housing costs in many suburban areas.* If no such standards existed, much less expensive new housing could be built there. How much less would new housing cost in that case? The answer depends upon how small the average new unit is, how well built it is, how much land it occupied, and where the land is in the metropolitan area. In Moscow, the average unit for a four-person household contains about 550 square feet—the same as a typical efficiency (no bedroom) apartment in the United States. In Britain, a two-bedroom unit occupies around 800 square feet—slightly less than the minimum FHA two-bedroom standard of around 850 square feet.[4] If we assume an average new unit size of 550 square feet for four persons, and a low construction cost of $11.50 per square foot, then a new unit would cost about $5,325 to build. If each unit occupied 1,100 square feet of land (twice its floor area), that would be a net residential density of 40 units per acre—typical of fairly dense garden apartments in the suburbs. If the land cost $4,000 per acre unimproved, or $24,000 per acre with all improvements, total land costs would be $600 per unit. Hence, the total cost of creating new housing with these relatively low quality standards would be about $7,000 per two-bedroom unit.

This is slightly less than 40 percent of the sales price of the least expensive new condominium townhouse or quadriplex units currently being marketed in most large metropolitan areas in the United States. It is about the same as the cost of a new average quality, single-wide mobile home—without land. In 1970, the proportion of all owner-occupied homes valued at under $7,500 by their owners was 5.7 percent in all American suburbs and 9.0 percent in all central cities.[5] Evidently, lowering quality standards to this extent (without abandoning them altogether) would cut the cost of new housing units about in half—and make them less expensive than most existing older units too. But it might also make those units seem unacceptably small to many American low-income households, whose housing tastes have been strongly influenced by mass media presentations featuring middle-class dwelling units. Nevertheless, these calculations indicate the degree to which current high housing costs are dependent upon our culturally determined quality standards rather than upon biologically determined shelter requirements.

Many suburbanites fear that a drastic reduction of quality standards for new housing might result in a burgeoning of "shanty towns" on the outskirts of our metropolitan areas. In fact, this has happened in nations where no minimum construction standards are enforced. So *some* minimum standards make sense. But they could be set much lower than those prevalent in many American areas, thereby greatly reducing the cost of new housing. If this is so, why do we have such high minimum standards?

Most people believe prevailing housing standards are based upon proven minimum requirements for a healthful or safe dwelling. But this is completely false. For example, no household "must have" a one-acre lot for healthful living, since millions of healthy Americans live on far smaller lots. In fact, there is no known, well-documented minimum lot size per household for healthful living. Thus, nearly all suburban minimum lot size requirements lack any relation whatever to health or safety needs. The same thing is true of minimum set-back and building placement requirements.

Prevailing structure type and minimum size requirements are also unsupported by any real data related to health needs. In fact, they are contradicted by a great deal of evidence. For example, most residential zoning regulations prohibit mobile homes. Yet there is absolutely no evidence that it is more healthful to live in a conventionally built home than in a mobile home. In Hong Kong, thousands of families live in publicly subsidized high-rise apartments containing only 280 square feet per unit. These families welcome living in what they regard as spacious and clean units—compared to the alternatives available.

Thus *all minimum size requirements and many construction method requirements incorporated in most suburban (and other) codes are based almost entirely upon cultural and even political considerations, not upon health or safety requirements.* This is true even though the basic legal justification for such ordinances—the police power—is founded on the community's right to protect its health and safety. I believe that prevailing minimum housing standards are really based upon four objectives of the people who already live in each community: (1) meeting their culturally conditioned (often social-class-related) perceptions of what is "desirable" or "socially acceptable"; (2) protecting their own property values; (3) avoiding certain consequences of higher density living, such as greater traffic congestion; and (4) excluding low- and moderate-income households by making local housing too expensive.

This procedure is certainly not a "natural" result of the market forces inherent in our free enterprise system. On the contrary, all legal minimum housing standards are direct interferences with free markets. Such standards abridge the rights of individual property owners to do what they choose with their properties. They also interfere with the rights of low- and moderate-income households both to choose freely where to live and to have reasonable access to job opportunities in the most dynamic portion of the economy. This means it is fallacious to attribute the "need" for housing subsidies solely to the low incomes of low- and moderate-income households. That "need" is also partly caused by political interference with free markets practiced by suburban residents to establish amenity levels they desire. Theoretically, those who benefit most from imposing high quality suburban housing standards should pay part of these housing subsidies.

That would help compensate the low- and moderate-income households whose freedoms are abridged by such high standards when no subsidies are made available.

Extra School Costs

Whenever a family moves into a suburb and sends several children to public schools, the increased expense of educating that family's children is larger than the local revenue gained from property taxes on its dwelling unit. This difference is partly offset by higher state aid to the school district because its attendance has gone up. But whenever a family's arrival raises total school expenses more than both local property tax revenue and state aid, that family has created a small "instant deficit." This results in higher taxes for all existing residents.

Such instant deficits can be caused by wealthy families as well as by poor ones. However, the greater the number of school-age children in the in-coming household, and the smaller the assessed value of its dwelling, the larger the instant deficit. Hence bigger *average* deficits are caused by low- and moderate-income households.

The tax raising impact of any one new household is very small per existing taxpayer. But the impact can become significant if many new households are involved.[6] Using nationwide average data for combined elementary and secondary per pupil expenditures, state aid, and local tax practices, I estimate that the average added tax burden of one more schoolchild upon local housing in 1970 was about $311. In order to generate added local school tax revenues of this amount, a new housing unit would have to have a market value of roughly $26,000. Thus, if a family with three schoolchildren moved into a school district and occupied a dwelling unit valued at $26,000, it would create an instant *residential* deficit of $622 per year. If 5,000 taxpaying households lived in the school district concerned, the increased taxes per household would be 12.4 cents per year, or only about four cents per child per year. But if 500 new households of this type moved into the district—a rise of only 10 percent in total households—the increased taxes would amount to $62 per year per original household. In many small suburbs, a single new subdivision can increase the number of schoolchildren by 30 to 100 percent. This often causes a big jump in the taxes of existing residents.

Similar instant deficits can also be generated by additional children entering schools from households already living in the district, whatever their incomes. For example, consider a family with two children in school and two preschool children, living in a home worth $52,000. When the two preschool children enter school, the household shifts to a net deficit position, thereby imposing higher taxes on all its neighbors (and itself).

Essentially, all children in public schools impose net tax burdens on others, because it costs more to educate them than the property they occupy adds to tax rolls. The difference in real property value between a housing unit occupied by a household with school-age children and one with the same income but no children represents the added property value "caused" by the children. It is rare that extra space needed for children adds as much as $26,000 per child to the market value of a housing unit. As a result, many suburbs are adopting zoning regulations aimed at preventing more school-age children from moving in. Some limit multifamily housing to efficiency and one-bedroom apartments. Others require huge minimum lot and building sizes to force single-family property values high enough to pay for any children sent to local schools. It is ironic that the very communities originally considered the ideal places to raise children are now trying to prevent entry of any more children.

This paradox suggests that it is fundamentally unsound to force those people who happen to own property in a community to pay for educating the children who happen to live there. Earlier in American history, when more families remained in one community most of their lives, each community was the main beneficiary of good education in its own schools. But during the past twenty-five years, an average of 20 percent of all Americans have changed residences *each year*— 13 percent within the same county, 3.5 percent to another county, and 3.5 percent to another state.[7] Therefore, social justice no longer requires that local residents pay most of the costs of educating the children living near them.

In many wealthier suburbs, parents want local school financing so they can provide expensive, high quality educations for their children. They fear that extension of the school tax base to a larger area would result in lower per pupil expenditures. Less affluent taxpayers politically dominant in any large area would resist high school costs. But the case for such economically based exclusion is much weaker regarding schools than regarding housing. Local public schools are not financed from voluntary expenditures in private markets, as is most housing. Rather, schools are paid for by taxes collected from *all* local residents—even those with no children—and spent by a public body. So parents seeking to maintain a high-cost school environment cannot logically screen out children from low- and moderate-income households, while admitting those from wealthier households, by invoking the principle of "individual household self-support." Very few households with children—no matter what their incomes— pay school property taxes large enough to cover all of even the locally financed costs of educating their children.

Moreover, provision of a "free" public education to all children residing within a given school district, regardless of their ability to pay, is a deeply entrenched American ideal. This contradicts the philosophy that only those people who pay the costs of maintaining high local standards should have access to the schools where those standards prevail. In fact, several courts have recently found the financing of schools mainly from local property taxes unconstitutional.[8] These decisions undermine the argument that individual communities have a right to exclude poor households in order to avoid the extra costs of educating children from those households.

OTHER SOCIAL SERVICES

Entry of low- and moderate-income households into middle- and upper-income suburbs would generate pressure for other public subsidies besides those for housing and schools. Such

households have certain needs, for which they have traditionally sought assistance from public agencies. Some of these
needs include:

1. Public transportation, especially local bus service
2. Income maintenance assistance, as in welfare programs
3. Family counseling
4. Manpower training programs
5. Locally administered unemployment compensation
   and counseling for the unemployed
6. Health care

In many suburban communities, the required services are
provided minimally or not at all.

Opening up the suburbs would cause many more affluent
communities to start bearing a fairer share of the costs of
providing these social services to poorer households. In this
respect, it would be a step toward achieving greater equality of
opportunity among urban Americans. We must recognize,
however, that the costs thereby shifted to suburban residents
(under present means of financing local governments) would
not be trivial.

Inadequacy of the Free Enterprise Approach

The basic *economic* rationale for excluding low- and moderate-income households from many suburban areas is what I
call the "free enterprise" argument: "We here in Goodlife
Acres have created high quality standards through our zoning
and building codes and public services because we have a right
to establish the kind of life style we want. Those standards
make living here more expensive, but we are paying to enjoy
that life style with our own hard-earned money. We do not get
subsidies from anyone else. So why should we be taxed to help
others enjoy this life style? Those who cannot afford it have no
right to expect us to help them. After all, in our free enterprise
society, they have the same opportunity to earn higher
incomes as we who have 'made it.' "

This argument is widely believed by American suburbanites. Yet it contains four fallacies or misleading implications.

1. *It is not true that most middle- and upper-income suburban households have not received public subsidies. All who own their own homes—and most do—receive a sizable housing subsidy right now.* The largest present housing subsidy consists of the federal income tax savings that owner-occupants of homes receive by deducting property taxes and mortgage interest from their taxable incomes. The United States Treasury estimates that this subsidy equaled about $5.7 billion in 1971 alone—more than *double* all other housing subsidies combined.[9] In 1966, owner-occupant families with incomes over $100,000 received an average benefit of $1,144 from this subsidy—or 18 times as much as the $64 average benefit received by owner-occupants with median incomes, and 381 times as much as that received by the poorest owner-occupant households. In fact, 69 percent of the total benefit was received by households with incomes of more than $10,000—the upper half of the income distribution.[10] This immense inequality is aggravated still further because renting households do not share in this subsidy; yet the proportion of renters is much higher among the poor.

Relatively affluent households also benefit from many other public subsidies, including oil depletion allowances, oil import quotas, lower borrowing rates because of federal mortgage guarantees, agricultural support programs,[11] real estate tax shelters, and tax-free municipal bonds. If public subsidies can be used to aid wealthy and middle-income suburban households, it is illogical and unfair to argue that the poor should enjoy only those privileges that they can fully pay for themselves. That is "socialism for the rich and free enterprise for the poor."

2. *It is not true that all American families have the same opportunity to earn high incomes, or that failure to earn a high income is caused mainly by unwillingness to work hard or to save.* Among the 25 million Americans officially defined as "poor" in 1970, at least 40 percent and perhaps over 50 percent could not possibly have earned enough income to escape from poverty through their own efforts. They were either too old, or disabled, or young

children, or mothers who had to take care of young children.[12] It seems unjust to make these citizens live in relative deprivation when their condition is not their own fault and when the rest of society is so well-off by comparison. Furthermore, the basic distribution of income in the United States tremendously favors the wealthy. It provides them with a degree of economic privilege that cannot plausibly be explained solely by their greater personal effort. In 1969, the lowest-income 20 percent of all families received only 5.6 percent of total family income before federal taxes. In contrast, the highest-income 20 percent received 41.0 percent of that total income.[13] Moreover, this unequal distribution had not changed much since 1947. True, taxes and transfer payments improve the relative economic position of the lowest-income groups. But they also pay the highest aggregate tax rates—when all local, state, and federal taxes are considered together.[14]

This suggests that the existing income distribution is greatly influenced by society's institutional structure—a conclusion that is reinforced by studies of social mobility and income changes from generation to generation. Christopher Jencks estimated that male workers whose parents were in the lowest 20 percent of the income distribution would earn an average of $6,076 in 1968; whereas those whose parents were in the upper 20 percent would earn an average of $10,800—or 78 percent more.[15] Although some of this inequality is attributable to differences in education and intelligence, the biggest single cause is that persons with identical education, intelligence scores, and occupations receive much higher pay if they come from high-status homes than if they come from low-status homes. Of course the children of the very wealthy usually have lower incomes than their parents, on the average, and the children of the very poor have higher incomes than their parents, on the average. Moreover, some people have risen from rags to riches through tremendous personal effort and ability, and the self-discipline and effort any household exhibits usually affect its standard of living to some degree. Yet on the average, the fact that some households have very low incomes and others have high incomes is significantly influenced by chance and by our basic social structure—not just by the relative merits and efforts of the individuals involved. So it is not true that everyone has an equal opportunity to earn his or her way into high-cost suburban areas.

3. *Communications in our society daily reveal to all citizens how well upper-middle-income groups live, and constantly urge everyone to live that way. In our democracy, it is unrealistic to expect the poor to accept their inferior lot under these conditions without seeking public aids to improve it.* Most Americans have relatively high living standards. This fact causes many of the poor to feel more deprived than their absolute condition would warrant if they did not realize how well-off the majority is. The communications media—especially television—serve to make the poor acutely aware of their relative deprivation. About 95 percent of even the poorest households in the country have television sets—in fact, a typical American child of eighteen has spent more hours watching television than attending school. A basic theme constantly reiterated by the media advertising paid for by supposedly conservative firms is that everyone ought to "live it up" by enjoying an extraordinary variety of benefits, regardless of his or her income. Another stimulant to the aspirations of the poor is the often repeated idea that the United States is an "affluent society," capable of solving almost any problem— as exemplified by our sending men to the moon and back.

All of these factors undermine the belief that only those who are well-off economically "deserve" to enjoy certain desirable standards of living. After all, most Americans accept the idea that *every* child has a right to a publicly financed education through high school. Most also believe that every citizen—rich or poor—has a right to personal protection by our system of justice. Many have extended this concept of "rights" to some degree of medical care. It is not a very big step to the argument that every household has a right to live in a good quality neighborhood even if it cannot pay all the costs of doing so itself. In fact, Congress has declared as an official national policy the "realization as soon as feasible . . . of a decent home and a suitable living environment for every American family," explicitly including those who are poor.

True, these factors tend to generate unrealistic aspirations among the poor. Our society cannot fulfill all those aspirations without immense changes in existing social priorities, if then. Furthermore, it is unwise and probably impossible to determine anyone's "rights" without simultaneously considering both his or her duties concerning them and who will pay the costs of providing those "rights." Nevertheless, it is just as futile to smugly defend existing inequalities by acting as though they resulted solely from differences in personal "merits" and as though the above factors stimulating discontent did not exist.

4. *It is not true that residents of any one part of a metropolitan area have an "absolute right" to determine living standards there without regard to the resulting impacts upon residents of other parts.* People in every part of each metropolitan area benefit from the contributions of others living in all other parts. Thus the concept of complete "local autonomy" or "local independence" implicit in the "free enterprise" argument is not valid. On the other hand, neither is it fair to completely submerge the interests and desires of people living in each part of the area to the requirements of the entire area.

In conclusion, I believe we must avoid two opposite but common fallacies concerning the economic costs of opening up the suburbs. Advocates of this policy often fail to recognize the large costs required. To argue that low- and moderate-income households have a right to enter suburban areas, without confronting the need to pay for that entry, is neither economically nor politically sound. But it is equally unsound to argue that no household should enter a suburban area unless it can bear the full costs of living there itself. The net result should be a dual recognition of the major costs of opening up the suburbs and of the need to pay some of them through public programs in order to achieve certain national objectives.

6 Neighborhood Linkages and Residential Exclusion

SOCIAL LINKAGES

The quality of life in every urban household is in part determined by the interactions of its members with other people in the vicinity of its dwelling unit. The most important of these are

1. *Personal movement* into, around, and out of the dwelling unit. Accomplishing this effectively requires personal safety and predictability of public comportment.
2. *Normal child play interactions.* Most parents want their children to play with other children who exhibit values, attitudes, and behavior patterns that will reinforce those the parents are trying to instill.
3. *School interactions.* In most areas, such interactions are linked to residence because school boundaries are based upon student attendance at the school nearest their homes.
4. *Direct environmental effects upon welfare.* These are aesthetic impacts of neighboring property maintenance, pollution from burning trash, and degree of messiness in the vicinity.
5. *Use of shared public facilities.* Examples are stores, churches, parks, and public transit vehicles. Efficiency of use requires personal safety and predictability of public comportment.

These interactions establish "external" or "spillover" effects that link the quality of life in each household to the behavior of other people living or working nearby. All urban households are affected by such linkages, so all are concerned about the behavior of their neighbors (and others who frequent the area).

The importance of external linkages can be reduced only by walling off individual households from others around them. This is a traditional practice in many Latin American and European cities, where housing often faces inward upon guarded courtyards and households have minimal contact with their neighbors. In American cities this practice is increasingly prevalent, as people chain their doors, stay off local streets, and live in high-rise buildings guarded by doormen, which are really vertical walled communities.

In contrast, two highly valued characteristics of suburban life are relative openness around each dwelling unit and fearless personal movement in each neighborhood. These advantages would be diminished if the external linkages in suburban neighborhoods were weakened. Hence most Americans would prefer enhancing the stability and effectiveness of such linkages.

How can this be done? One way is to increase the effectiveness of social controls upon individual behavior. Then each household could normally expect its neighbors, no matter who they were, to observe certain fundamental rules promoting personal security. For many reasons, the effectiveness of all kinds of social controls appears to have been declining recently. Moreover, it is hard to imagine how this trend can soon be reversed.

In fact, we must recognize that many American households do not exhibit or uphold the standards of public behavior, personal safety, morals, language, or private behavioral codes considered minimally acceptable by sizable groups in our population—even by the majority. Much of the "nonconforming" behavior of these households is a matter of personal style—as in their language and relatively unrestrained public comportment. But other nonconforming behavior creates serious consequences that almost all groups in our society consider very undesirable. Examples are frequent resort to violence, destructiveness toward property, lack of respect for the rights and privacy of others, and proclivity toward theft. It must be emphasized that only a small minority of all low-income households exhibit such behavior. Most poor households—white, black, or other—have the same values and behavior patterns as most middle-income households but less money. Moreover, as I stated earlier, I believe that even those low-income households who exhibit seriously negative behavior patterns have basic values and aspirations very similar to those of most middle-income Americans. Their behavior consists of various adaptations to their continual experiences of failure, which have convinced them that they cannot achieve the typical aspirations of most Americans through conforming behavior. Since these repeated failures are caused in part by institutional and social arrangements beyond their own control, it is usually unjust to blame these households for their negative behavior. But it is equally unjust to ignore the impacts of that behavior upon others or to condemn those others for trying to protect themselves from its very real negative consequences.

Nonconforming households pose a potential threat to neighborhoods occupied primarily by households who conform to the public behavior patterns accepted by most Americans. Without effective means of changing the behavior of nonconforming households, the conforming ones can maintain their quality of life in only two ways. One is to prevent the entry of many nonconforming households into their neighborhoods. The other is to move to where few nonconforming households are present. But many households do not want to bear the costs of moving in order to protect the quality of life in their neighborhoods, especially if they have made large fixed investments to create a good quality of life at their present location. Given this outlook, only residential exclusion can maintain the local quality of life these households desire.

Such exclusion forms a second method of enhancing the neighborhood linkages described above. As noted earlier, every urban household is necessarily concerned with its neighbors' behavior—particularly with their public comportment and the way they maintain and use the property they occupy. Therefore, it is reasonable for each household to want to exclude from its neighborhood people whose behavior would seriously deteriorate its own quality of life. This means that *residential discrimination of some type among urban households is an inevitable characteristic of effective urban living.* The word *discrimination* as used here certainly does *not* mean racial or ethnic discrimination. It means making distinctions among people on the basis of traits that are truly relevant to legitimate human purposes.

THE LEGITIMACY OF SOME EXCLUSION

Some Americans contend that *any* attempt to influence the behavior of one's neighbors is a violation of the neighbors' individual rights. According to this view, the mores and standards of all groups in society have equal value and validity; hence no one group—including the middle-class majority—can legitimately impose its standards upon others. Any attempts to do so should be struck down as illegal.

A less extreme view—and one I believe valid—is that residential exclusion ostensibly performed to protect the local environment denies equal opportunity to members of the excluded groups. When nearly every suburb decides to "protect the quality of its own environment" by excluding relatively low-cost housing, then almost all poor households are denied equal access to suburban jobs and schools. Society should not remain blind to this outcome. Moreover, since exclusion from better schooling and employment opportunities keeps low- and moderate-income households from acquiring the very attributes the excluding persons so admire, this is a self-perpetuating condemnation.

At the other extreme are those who believe that individual rights *require* the power to carry out residential exclusion. They argue that such rights are meaningless unless a group of like-minded people can get together and establish the local environmental quality they prefer. They must then be able to defend it from change by preventing the entry of others whose presence would alter it. In defense of this view they cite two basic values: the nature of private property and the determination of neighborhood quality by the *community* rather than by the *individual*.

The power of exclusion is an essential characteristic of private property. The saying, "A man's home is his castle," implies that each man has the right to exclude anyone from his home. Exercising this power does not mean placing the *property* rights of the occupant over the *personal* rights of those seeking entry. Any household's personal rights to privacy are meaningless unless they can be exercised over some physical space. And without the right to privacy, most other personal rights (such as free speech) are seriously weakened. So personal rights are inextricably related to property rights. True, every society suspends a household's right to exclude others under certain circumstances. For example, the police can legally enter a private home with a warrant. But this does not alter the normal dominance of the principle that any household should be able to exclude others from its home.

But where does its "home" end? The quality of every household's home life is seriously affected by events occurring outside its dwelling unit but nearby. To make the sanctity of the home effective, therefore, households must have some right to influence the quality of their neighborhoods, too. From this *community* aspect of *individual* rights, defenders of residential exclusion argue that any group of citizens ought to be able to establish a physical enclave where certain standards of environmental quality and behavior are required for all residents. The resulting exclusion of those too poor to meet the standards is considered essential to protect the rights of those who established the standards.

RECONCILING THE EXTREMES

I believe resolution of the views stated above should be based upon the following principles:

1. Every household must recognize that it has certain social obligations and responsibilities as well as certain individual rights.

2. The quality of life of every individual household depends greatly upon the quality of life in its community—that is, upon how its neighbors behave concerning certain key inter-

personal relations. Therefore, every household has a right to be concerned with certain vital aspects of its neighbors' behavior.

3. No individual household or group of neighboring households can establish a reasonably peaceful and safe local environment unless it can effectively prevent certain types of behavior in its neighborhood. This requires either preventing such behavior on the part of households already living there, or preventing households likely to exhibit such behavior from living there at all.

4. The degree of exclusion any household has a right to exercise is greatest within the physical boundaries of its dwelling unit and declines as distance from those boundaries increases.

5. The only legitimate reason for excluding any households from a residential neighborhood is that their presence would seriously reduce the quality of life of those living there by affecting the external linkages described earlier. However, "quality of life" is an ambiguous concept that changes meaning over time. Clearly defining this principle in practical terms is therefore extremely difficult.

6. The right of any group to establish standards that exclude others from its neighborhood must be balanced with the right of those others to enjoy access to certain basic opportunities in society. Neither of these rights can be considered unconditional; each must be exercised in light of its overall impact upon the other. In practice, this means that different degrees of residential exclusion may be practiced at different geographic scales. This is explored in chapter 10.

7. No one has a right to exclude others from a neighborhood because of factors that have no functional relationship to the basic quality of community life (such as race or ethnic origin). Opinions differ about what characteristics significantly affect the quality of community life. Some people, for example, want to exclude all high-density housing from their neighborhoods because they view the traffic movement and congestion required for such housing as undesirable.

8. Particular means used to carry out neighborhood exclu-

sion should not generate costs for households whose behavior does not pose any threat to the quality of life in the areas concerned. An exclusionary mechanism is "efficient" in this sense only if it has two characteristics. First, it must exclude a very *high* proportion of all the households whose behavior would truly reduce the quality of life in the area. Second, it must exclude a very *low* proportion of households whose behavior would *not* reduce the quality of life in the area. It is doubtful that excluding households mainly on the basis of their incomes is efficient in either way.

7 Sources of Opposition

At present, millions of Americans oppose opening up the suburbs. There are eight main sources of this opposition: three economic, four social, and one political. In this chapter I will briefly mention those discussed earlier and analyze the others in more detail. The analysis is aimed at understanding both why such opposition arises and how the concerns it expresses might be met in ways that would not impede opening up the suburbs.

RESISTANCE TO RISING LOCAL PROPERTY TAXES

Movement of low- and moderate-income households into suburban areas might raise the property taxes of households already living there. Naturally, most existing residents oppose this, as discussed in chapter 5.

RESISTANCE TO HIGHER FEDERAL TAXES FOR HOUSING SUBSIDIES

Many suburbs do not permit building or maintaining relatively low quality (and therefore lower cost) housing; so most low- and moderate-income households cannot afford to live there without direct government subsidies. Suburban residents may resist entry of such households because they do not want to pay higher federal taxes to finance those subsidies.

Also, many suburban taxpayers would resent apparent "inequities" caused by direct housing subsidies. For example, assume Jones owns a house on which he pays high taxes and receives no *obvious* subsidies. He may be infuriated when he realizes that his federal taxes are helping his poorer neighbor Smith live in an identical house at much lower cost, even though Smith pays much lower income taxes. As discussed in chapter 5, this "inequity" arises partly because Jones and his neighbors have passed laws preventing Smith from building a new home he can afford. Moreover, Jones receives a hidden housing subsidy through income tax deductions. The subtleties of these arguments are not likely to impress Jones, however, when he looks at his neighbor's new home.

FEAR OF FALLING PROPERTY VALUES

Many Americans believe that entry of *any* poor households into a middle-income neighborhood immediately causes a decline in property values. Whether this is true is not really known, since little research has been done on the subject. However, when many people speak of "low-income households" moving into an area, they really mean "black households." At least their conclusions about the impact of the former stem from their beliefs about the impact of the latter.

The effect upon property values of black households entering an all-white neighborhood has been scientifically studied several times.[1] Property values can move either up or down compared to values in similar areas not so affected, depending upon the particular circumstances. Unfortunately, that is not very comforting for a family that believes the value of its biggest single asset—its home—is threatened by entry of low- and moderate-income households. This widespread belief is based upon experience in areas undergoing massive population transition, which are usually located on the edges of large economic or ethnic "ghettos." Entry of a few members of the ethnic minority almost invariably signals the beginning of a steady transition toward predominant occupancy by members of that minority.

In the long run, I believe, such "massive transition" of an entire neighborhood from mainly middle-income households (whether white or black) to mainly low-income households (whether white or black) usually produces a decline in average property values, for there is much less total income in the area after such a transition than before. If the poorer households try to make up for lower incomes by doubling up occupancy, this raises maintenance costs or causes faster deterioration. Even if the poorer households spend higher fractions of their incomes on housing, they are unlikely to attain the same spending levels as before. More important, the resale market for local housing also shifts from middle-income to lower-income households, who cannot afford to pay as much.

However, the situation of such an older middle-income neighborhood on the edge of a large low-income area is vastly different from that of a typical suburban middle-income area. Because the latter is far removed from the nearest low-income "ghetto," it is not under constant, intensive pressure for "takeover." A significant number of low- and moderate-income households (white or black) can enter without being followed by thousands more. There need be no decline in property values in such a neighborhood as a whole.

The key to keeping up property values in any neighborhood is maintaining its desirability as a place to live in the minds of other households who do not live there now but who constitute the broad general market for housing of that type in the metropolitan area. This "absentee market" contains the potential buyers and renters of housing units that become available through normal population turnover. Each year about 20 percent of all American households move; so one out of every five housing units in the average neighborhood becomes available annually. Thus "neighborhood stability" does not mean that the same people live in an area year after year. Rather, it means that the type of household moving in is about the same as the type moving out.

Similarly, stability of property values in an area means that the people living elsewhere who seriously consider moving in have about the same purchasing power as those already living there and consider the neighborhood just as desirable—relative to others—as it was when the present residents moved in. Property values fall when there is a major shift in the nature or beliefs of this potential market. The people living in the area can contribute to such a shift if they complain that the area is deteriorating or is likely to do so. Potential residents now living elsewhere will learn of this view and will downgrade the area's desirability in their own minds. This will reduce property values, because those values are determined by what the potential buyers and renters are willing to pay.

Under these nearly universal circumstances, three conditions are necessary to maintain a middle-income area's
desirability *after* low- and moderate-income households have
begun to move in:

1. There must be no perceptible rise in crime rates,
   vandalism, property deterioration, or other signs of
   decline.
2. There must be a widespread belief that the future
   percentage of low- and moderate-income households
   will not rise above some "tipping point."
3. The entry of such households must not make this area
   so different from other similar neighborhoods in the
   same metropolitan area that it becomes relatively less
   desirable than before.

The last two conditions require further discussion.

The concept of a *racial* "tipping point" is a familiar one, but
the concept of an *economic* "tipping point" is relatively
unexplored. I believe that entry of low- and moderate-income
households into a predominantly middle-income area will
indeed cause a decline in property values unless the absentee
market is convinced that this entry will culminate in a stable
minority percentage of such households in the area. This belief
will cause the middle-class absentee market to *think* that the
area will retain the predominantly middle-class atmosphere its
members strongly desire. Then households in that market will
keep moving in—thereby confirming their own opinion.
Clearly, the views the absentee market holds about a neighborhood's future constitute a self-fulfilling prophecy. Those
views determine the behavior of that market, which in turn
determines the future composition of the neighborhood.

Under these conditions, property values in any middle-income area would be much easier to maintain if there were
some means of "guaranteeing" that the percentage of low- and
moderate-income households living there would not exceed a
stated maximum well below 50 percent. This implies that
some sort of economic quota system would be effective in
helping to maintain property values, for it would strongly

affect the opinions of the absentee market about the area's future.

Even when no such guarantee exists, several factors can help sustain belief in continued future middle-income dominance in an area. The likelihood of "massive transition" ending such dominance in any neighborhood is lower

1. The farther the neighborhood is from any large existing concentration of low-income housing
2. The smaller the initial concentration of low- and moderate-income households is in any one part of the neighborhood
3. The more the new set of low- and moderate-income housing units in the neighborhood is tightly surrounded by well-established high-value housing or institutions or physical barriers
4. The lower the fraction of low- and moderate-income children is in the area's elementary and secondary schools
5. The closer the neighborhood is to some outstanding amenity sustaining middle-income housing demand there, such as a major university, a lakefront, or a large park

It is really the *relative* desirability of any neighborhood that influences its absentee market. For example, assume that low- and moderate-income households began to enter only one middle-income suburban area in a metropolitan region containing one hundred such neighborhoods. That area would become less desirable in the eyes of many potential middle-income residents. Why should they run *any* risks—however small—of declining property values or other possible drawbacks when they have ninety-nine other areas to choose from that do not require such risk-taking? Now assume that all one hundred neighborhoods started receiving about the same percentage of low- and moderate-income residents simultaneously. Then potential middle-income buyers or renters could not escape living with low- and moderate-income households. They would have no alternatives except leaving the metropolitan area altogether. This would almost totally eliminate risks of declining property values caused by the entry of low- and moderate-income households in *any* of the one hundred neighborhoods.

In reality, no policies can introduce the same fraction of low- and moderate-income households everywhere in suburbia at once. But this example illustrates how vital it is to open up as widely spread a group of suburbs as possible in a metropolitan area almost simultaneously, rather than concentrating on opening up only a few portions at a time. Such broad dispersal is the best way to protect each individual neighborhood from adverse effects to property value. Unfortunately, no mechanisms presently exist that can ensure such an outcome. That is why fear of declining property values is a major source of opposition to opening up the suburbs—especially near each specific location where low- and moderate-income housing is proposed.

Fear of Rising Crime and Vandalism Rates

Many people move to suburbs to escape certain undesirable aspects of big-city life. These include high crime rates, high personal insecurity, low quality public schools, lack of open space, and a general sense of congestion. It is easy to understand why they strongly oppose policies they believe would bring into their suburban sanctuaries the very conditions they sought to escape. Since they associate high crime and vandalism rates with low-income households, they are opposed to opening the suburbs to such households. Many whites associate high crime rates with blacks; so they are doubly fearful of having low- and moderate-income black households as neighbors.

It is both inaccurate and unwise to dismiss these widespread beliefs as mere prejudice. There is overwhelming statistical evidence that high crime, vandalism, and delinquency rates are indeed found in areas that are predominantly low-income or predominantly black—and especially both.[2] The vast majority of middle-income Americans are well aware of these facts. Therefore their fears must be confronted directly. People have a right to be concerned about the behavior of others living near them.

As I have noted before, even in crisis ghettos, most low-income households are not the perpetrators of crime but its victims. Though crime rates are high there, only a minority of the residents actually commit crimes or exhibit what most Americans would consider undesirable behavior. So it is both statistically and morally wrong to conclude that all or even a majority of low- and moderate-income households—white or black—would create undesirable behavior patterns if they moved into a middle-income area.

But it is very difficult—perhaps impossible—to know in advance whether the particular group of low- and moderate-income households likely to move into any specific neighborhood will contain a significant percentage of the destructive minority that exhibits undesirable behavior. The relevant question is thus whether entry of low- and moderate-income households to predominantly middle-income areas not adjacent to low-income ghettos would cause undesirable behavior patterns to appear.

It must be remembered that *there is a vast difference between a neighborhood in which poverty is dominant and one in which it is present to a minor degree but in which middle-income conditions are dominant.* The high crime, vandalism, and delinquency rates in low-income areas are caused to a great extent by the pervasive economic deprivation there. Destructive behavior in individual households is intensified when it also exists in many other households nearby. Furthermore, neighborhood institutions in crisis ghettos debilitate individual households by exploiting and encouraging their weaknesses while providing minimal support to their strengths. Examples are retail stores that charge exorbitantly for credit purchases, drug pushers, numbers racketeers, and street gangs. It is quite possible that many middle- and upper-income suburbs would not offer much help to newly arriving low- and moderate-income households with problems. But at least the community would not surround them with an exploitative environment. It might also support their positive traits and help to counteract negative ones. And perhaps the presence of new households in need of personal assistance would encourage many suburban families to develop more supportive interactions with their neighbors.

It is easy to exaggerate both the amount of help low- and moderate-income households need and the virtues of middle-income communities. Most low- and moderate-income households do not suffer from any inherent deficiencies; they just lack money. If they had the financial resources to live in suburban areas, they would do so in what middle-income Americans would regard as a "desirable" manner. Moreover, plenty of undesirable behavior patterns are found in middle-income suburban America, including alcoholism, various neuroses, intrafamily hostilities, white-collar crimes, racism, and a widespread lack of empathy. Yet no realistic approach to any urban policies can ignore the fact that many poor households suffer from serious problems in addition to lack of money. Some problems are just dysfunctional, such as low quality education and lack of employable skills. But there is also clear evidence that most social and individual pathologies are more common among the poor than in any other income group. As a result, many poor households need some kind of community help to cope with their problems. And because failure to cope often produces adverse consequences not only for the families themselves but for their neighbors, any program of opening up the suburbs should include ways to help such households deal with these difficulties successfully.

Moreover, any such program must realistically answer the question of whether entry of low- and moderate-income households to a predominantly middle-income suburban area will introduce more crime, vandalism, and delinquency. The answer depends upon four factors: (1) whether the *proportion* of low- and moderate-income households can be kept low enough so middle-income attitudes and behavior remain dominant, (2) whether the community will provide positive support—psychological as well as financial—for poorer households and the services they need, (3) the specific geographic location patterns of such households in the areas concerned and (4) whether such households are initially screened so as to limit the percentage of multiproblem households among those entering middle-income areas. These factors are discussed further in chapters 9, 10, and 12.

FEAR OF A DECLINE IN THE QUALITY OF SCHOOLS

Millions of Americans have moved to the suburbs to provide their children with better public schooling than they believed was available in central cities. For nearly *all* middle-class American households with school-age children, regardless of race or nationality, choosing a place to live is greatly influenced by school quality. These parents believe formal education is vital to their children's eventual economic and personal success. They also believe the social interaction among children in and around schools has a strong impact on their children's values and attitudes. Schools are relevant to residential choices because where the household lives usually determines what school its children attend, what school taxes it pays, and what is taught in those schools.

Middle-class parents judge the quality of any school mainly in terms of the kinds of families whose children predominate there. Those families are usually appraised in terms of their incomes and their ethnic character (including both race and nationality), and sometimes in terms of their religion. These family characteristics are considered far more important than the nature of the school's physical plant, the technical qualifications of its teachers, or even expenditures per pupil.

Parents perceived the crucial importance of students' family backgrounds in determining educational quality long before the Coleman report or the recent research of Christopher Jencks and his colleagues. This perception stemmed from the importance parents place upon the social interaction in schools and its impact upon the values and attitudes of their children. Typical middle-class parents the world over want school classmates to support and thereby reinforce the values and attitudes they have been teaching their children at home. They assume—I believe correctly—that other children will provide such value reinforcement if those children come from homes whose adults are like themselves. Hence, the widespread desire of middle-class parents to establish social homo-geneity in their neighborhoods results from their value-rein-forcing objectives concerning the school experience of their children. Other reasons why middle-class households choose homes in relatively homogeneous neighborhoods were dis-cussed in chapter 6.

Thus, most American middle-class parents try to send their children to schools that are attended predominantly by children from other families with the same or better socioeco-nomic backgrounds than their own. However, there are many different levels of economic and social status within the American middle class. So each household's search for areas where people are of the same or "higher" status produces a number of different residential strata.

Some parents also believe that religion is a key factor. Around 40 percent of all Catholic parents achieve religious value reinforcement for their children by supporting separate private schools (at the elementary level).[3] Many Jewish parents seek cultural-religious dominance in public schools by residing in clusters so their children dominate the neighbor-hood schools.

Race and color are also considered important to school homogeneity by many parents. Probably a majority of white parents believe their children should not attend schools in which blacks, Puerto Ricans, or other minority-group children constitute a large enough percentage to prevent dominance by white students in most aspects of school life. This attitude may change in the future as a result of large-scale racial integration of schools, especially in the South, but I believe it is still prevalent. Undoubtedly, it is partly based upon sheer preju-dice. But it also occurs because many whites associate certain traits widely considered undesirable with membership in specific minority groups. Most middle-class whites know that a relatively high proportion of urban blacks, Puerto Ricans, and Mexican Americans live in low-income households. They also know that predominantly low-income urban areas exhibit high rates of crime, vandalism, delinquency, drug addiction, illegitimate births, and broken families. Moreover, they know these conditions influence the environment within schools serving such areas. But many middle-class whites fail to recognize that these undesirable traits are *not* exhibited by most of the members of these ethnic groups or by most low-income households, so they erroneously conclude that these undesirable traits are inherently related either to poverty or to membership in certain ethnic minority groups.

Other whites who realize that no such inherent relationship exists nevertheless fear the entry of either poor or ethnic minority households into their areas and their local schools. The *probability* that any group of newcomers to their neighborhoods or schools will exhibit certain undesirable traits is much higher, it seems to them, if those persons are poor or members of certain ethnic minorities than if they are not. This inference is difficult to disprove statistically, even though I think it rests upon two false assumptions. One is that any group of newcomers who are either poor or members of these ethnic minorities will contain the same percentage of persons exhibiting undesirable traits as prevails in crisis ghettos. The other is that people will behave in exactly the same manner in a predominantly middle-income area and its schools as in the exploitative, deprived environment of the ghetto. At present, a great many middle-class white households believe these assumptions about both poor and minority-group households. In selecting schools, as a result, they impute importance to relative ethnic homogeneity as well as to economic homogeneity—just like other white middle-class parents motivated by sheer prejudice. Moreover, many black middle-class households hold these same assumptions about low-income households, so they resist entry of poor households into their own neighborhoods and schools.

Whichever factors are concerned, almost all middle-class parents of all races want their children to attend schools where some screening of students has occurred to prevent dominance by those who possess characteristics they regard as undesirable. Moreover, as noted above, many middle-class parents associate certain undesirable traits with children from lower income households. Therefore, they do not want many such children to attend school with their own children. They fear that opening up the suburbs might lead to their schools being "flooded" with children from such households. This fear is reinforced by past experience in central-city neighborhoods undergoing "massive" transition. They believe such "flooding" would end the dominance of middle-class values in their schools, and therefore destroy what they regard as one of the most important functions of public schools.

However, these parents do not necessarily demand total exclusion of students from low-income households. Their purposes can be achieved if just enough exclusion occurs to ensure predominance of the values, attitudes, and behavior patterns they approve. Thus *some* entry of low-income and even "undesirable" students can occur in schools serving their neighborhoods without significantly impairing attainment of their educational objectives.

Desire to Maintain "Social Distance"

Social class and status are important everywhere in the world to some degree. In the United States, it is hard to perceive exactly where boundaries between social classes are located or who possesses any particular status. This ambiguity poses a psychological threat to those trying to show others— and themselves—that they have definitely "arrived" at a certain status. Such people frequently try to distinguish themselves sharply and visibly from others who they believe have lower status. At one time this could be done through personal appearance. But our era provides cheap mass production of clothing, rapid copying of "exclusive" designs, and highly individualized styles. Even conspicuous consumer items like sports cars and stereos have been widely copied in inexpensive versions. However, where one lives is still a clearly visible symbol of social status too expensive to duplicate easily. As American households gain more income, they typically move from one neighborhood to another, each fancier than the last, rather than upgrading their homes in one place. Consequently, most residential neighborhoods are widely perceived as having definite social status, and this perception directly affects property values.

Families who have recently escaped from relative poverty are especially anxious to establish a clear "social distance" between themselves and those supposedly of lower status. An effective way to do this is by moving into neighborhoods where the poor clearly cannot afford to live. Similarly, many white households want to maintain physical separation from black households to reinforce their "superiority" to the latter in their own minds.

These psychological factors provide a powerful—though often unconscious—reason for many households to oppose opening up their neighborhoods to poorer families. I recognize that attaining some degree of status is psychologically important for everyone. But I do not believe it is legitimate to do so by denying equal opportunities to others, especially when public powers are involved. Hence I do not believe social policies should be shaped to serve this status-differentiating motive.

CENTRAL-CITY FEARS OF LOSS OF LEADERS

Surprisingly, some central-city leaders oppose opening up the suburbs, too. They fear that the low- and moderate-income households most likely to leave central cities would be those with the most stability, initiative, and ambition. The departure of these "high quality" poor households would leave an even greater concentration of multiproblem households in central cities. This would reduce the ability of poverty neighborhoods there to improve themselves by developing indigenous leaders.

It is probably true that the low- and moderate-income households most likely to take advantage of suburban opportunities would be those with the greatest ambition and stability. Yet failure to provide them with any real choice of living in the suburbs is penalizing them for being ambitious and stable. Should we create indigenous leaders for poverty areas by preventing those who want to leave from doing so? That is the implication of the above argument.

Nevertheless, this argument calls attention to a crucial but largely ignored question concerning all urban affairs: *how does our society intend to cope with the poorest, least competent, least educated, least skilled, and most problem-ridden households in our urban areas?* These households generate a disproportionate percentage of urban crimes, drug addiction, mental illness, vandalism, juvenile delinquency, illegitimacy, welfare costs, unemployment, and housing abandonment. Undoubtedly, their doing so is caused mainly by social and institutional forces beyond their own control—I am not trying to "blame" them. Yet neither do I believe it is fruitful to ignore their role in causing these conditions for fear of being accused of racial or social-class prejudice.

Most schemes of urban development—including many proposed in this book—deal mainly with nonproblem households. For example, some educators think that creating a classroom environment favorable to learning implies limiting the proportion of children from "culturally deprived" homes. But in areas where they are the majority, where will the children be educated, and how? In our largest cities, thousands of such households are concentrated in the poorest neighborhoods. How can we help them overcome the resulting environment dominated by deprivation? We are devoting far too little energy and resources to answering this crucial question. It is discussed further in later chapters.

THE BLACK NATIONALIST POSITION

One argument against opening up the suburbs is that blacks as a group can maximize their future political power by remaining concentrated within central cities. In many cities, the black population already constitutes a high enough percentage of the total to exert significant political influence. If many blacks move into suburbs, the political impact of continued black concentration in central cities will be reduced. Yet the political power of the blacks in suburbia will be nullified by vast white majorities there. This argument is usually directed against racial integration rather than against economic integration, but blacks comprise a significant fraction of the low- and moderate-income households in our largest metropolitan areas, so movement of large numbers of low- and moderate-income households to the suburbs would involve quite a few blacks.

Nevertheless, at least for the near future, this argument poses a false dilemma between increasing black political power and providing greater suburban housing choices to blacks. As long as the amount of black out-movement to the suburbs is relatively modest—which it surely would be at the beginning of an economic integration strategy—there would still be a strong central-city power base for the black community in many large cities. Black outflows to the suburbs might slow the growth of the central-city black population, but they would probably not cause any decline in its size. Moreover, the political power of that population could be enhanced much more in the short run by better organization than by increased size.

In the long run, there probably would be some trade off between maximizing black political power in central cities and achieving more racial integration in the suburbs. Yet I believe it is in the best interests of both black and white Americans to attain as much suburban racial integration as possible. This is desirable to avoid the type of potential spatial/racial confrontation between mostly poor, mostly black inner cities and mostly affluent, almost entirely white suburbs deplored by the National Advisory Commission on Civil Disorders. It is true that scattered black suburbanites could not amass as much direct elective power as they might if concentrated together as part of a larger central-city voting bloc. Yet the presence of at least some black residents in most suburban areas would greatly reduce the probability that white suburbanites would define suburban interests in ways that are antiblack as well as anti-central-city. Black suburbanites would be able to exercise at least some beneficial influence that would not arise if nearly all urban blacks remained in central cities. Their presence would also keep open a much broader set of residential and employment choices to future black citizens. In my opinion, those goals are worth the sacrifice of marginal increases in black central-city power required to achieve meaningful racial integration in the suburbs.

8 Preliminary Conditions of Reconciliation

The preceding chapters have presented an apparently irreconcilable conflict between two major groups in American society. On one hand, millions of presently deprived low- and moderate-income Americans are seeking to upgrade themselves by escaping from conditions of poverty. Such upgrading is clearly in the mainstream of American tradition. But achieving it will require entry of many low- and moderate-income households into residential areas now occupied almost exclusively by middle- and upper-income groups.

On the other hand, the middle class wants to protect the quality of life it has won through past striving and effort. Such protection is equally in the mainstream of American tradition. But to achieve it, middle- and upper-income households must exclude many low- and moderate-income households from presently middle-class neighborhoods.

The best way to resolve the conflict is to devise specific arrangements that allow both groups to achieve simultaneously most of their legitimate objectives. I believe such arrangements are practically attainable. Achieving them will require most members of both groups to agree upon the following basic "rules of the game" for effective urban policy-making:

1. Both low- and moderate-income households seeking entry into suburban areas and middle- and upper-income households seeking to protect the quality of their neighborhood environments must recognize the legitimacy of the other group's basic goals. This should be easy, since both are trying to attain decent housing, good jobs, good schooling for their children, safe neighborhoods, and healthful environments.

2. Both groups must be willing to compromise by accepting

outcomes that achieve the most essential aspects of their own goals but not all aspects.

3. Americans must recognize that certain individual and property rights can be achieved only at the neighborhood or community level. This often requires restriction of the purely individual rights of some persons or households. Some desirable neighborhood conditions require "balanced mixtures" of different kinds of people. These conditions cannot be attained by either the complete exclusion from the area, or the complete admission into it, of specific kinds of people. Hence not all individuals with the same characteristics would always be treated equally.

4. All citizens must recognize that each metropolitan area is socially and economically unified; so its residents are interdependent parts of a single whole. Therefore, it is both factually and ethically wrong for residents of any one part to believe they can behave "autonomously" in relation to all or any of the other parts.

5. If a preponderant majority of Americans strongly desire certain basically legitimate social objectives, public policies running counter to that desire are not likely to work effectively—especially if they require major changes in existing institutions. The majority will be able to evade or nullify the effects of those policies under most circumstances. The legislative and administrative branches of government in a democracy are powerfully motivated to serve any desire strongly held by a majority of their constituents. Also, in the United States, a majority of citizens are in the middle class. They have enough money and political skills to evade policies they passionately oppose. Therefore, if public policies are to be effective, they should not usually seek to prevent a preponderant majority from achieving any of its strongly favored objectives.

6. On the other hand, the protection of certain individual rights vital to our democratic society sometimes requires courts to enforce public policies that a majority oppose. A viable democracy is based upon two principles that, if carried to

extremes, can become inconsistent or even contradictory.[1] One is majority rule, which operates through elections and other decision-making based upon voting. The other is that individuals have certain inalienable rights that should be protected at all times—even from the actions of a majority. There is always some "frontier of tension" between these two principles in a democracy. In American government, federal courts are the main protectors of individual rights. They are not as dependent upon approval of a majority of some constituency as are legislative and executive bodies. This means that court action must play a crucial role in creating those social changes necessary to protect individual rights against adverse majority desires.

True, there are limits to how far federal courts can go in stimulating social change beyond the current views of a majority of voters. Congress can remove certain subjects from normal court jurisdiction or adopt new laws designed to circumvent court rulings or even initiate Constitutional amendments to counteract unpopular court decisions. The president can alter the composition of the federal courts over time if he strongly disapproves of their rulings. Nevertheless, the role of courts in stimulating social change is particularly vital because few major social institutions ever make basic changes in their own behavior or structures through purely internal developments. Such changes almost always result from external pressures or changes in their outside environments.

If most Americans in metropolitan areas accept the above conditions, I believe specific public policies can be designed and adopted that would effectively open up the suburbs. The substance of such policies should be based upon the concepts described in the next chapters.

9   The Viability of Neighborhoods

American experience has taught us two lessons underlying the key conclusions of this book. The first is that *most urban neighborhoods containing relatively high concentrations of low-income households are neither economically nor socially viable.* They do not provide reasonably decent, safe, and healthful living environments. On the contrary, poverty-dominated environments breed conditions that perpetuate poverty among the residents, drive out most households who can afford to move elsewhere, and adversely affect surrounding areas.

The second lesson is that *both the upgrading desired by low- and moderate-income households and the protection of neighborhood quality desired by middle- and upper-income households can be achieved simultaneously in the same neighborhoods if a significant number of low- and moderate-income households live there, providing that middle-class dominance is maintained.* "Middle-class dominance" means that the preponderant majority of persons living in a neighborhood or interacting in most institutions serving it (such as public schools) are from middle- and upper-income households. A "preponderant majority" is a sufficiently high percentage (well over 50 percent) so that middle-class mores and behavior remain prevalent.

From these two lessons comes the following corollary: *in most cases, keeping an urban neighborhood economically and socially viable requires maintaining middle-class dominance there.* This does not mean that predominantly low-income areas can never be viable or that all middle-class dominated areas are viable. But it does imply that neighborhood viability is normally linked with middle-class dominance and is difficult to maintain without it.

DEFINING NEIGHBORHOOD VIABILITY

Common to all of the many definitions of the term *neighborhood* is the idea that people living in the same neighborhood continually interact with one another in their daily lives. The size of the area considered a "neighborhood" is thus related to the types of daily interaction relevant to the analysis. In normal residential living, the key interactions are those described in chapter 6. These generate the following different scales of "neighborhood": the small cluster of housing in the immediate vicinity of any dwelling unit (derived mainly from normal play interactions of children); the multiblock grouping of housing units built and marketed by a single developer (found mainly in suburbs); the multiblock grouping of housing units with approximately the same basic spatial relationship to surrounding physical barriers and public transit systems (found mainly in larger cities); the elementary school attendance area; and the commercial trade area served primarily by a single set of convenience goods stores. Consumers in housing markets usually behave as though one or more of the last four definitions were most relevant, so any of those could be used. For convenience, I will use the elementary school attendance area as equivalent to a neighborhood, and I will arbitrarily assume that the average urban elementary school contains 750 students, making the total population of the average urban "neighborhood" approximately 5,000 persons. I will use other sizes when data for this type of neighborhood are lacking.

I define a neighborhood as *viable* if it would be considered a reasonably decent, safe, and healthful living environment for families with children if judged by the standards currently held by a majority of Americans. It is hard to define those standards precisely, especially since they change over time. But a viable neighborhood should exhibit the following characteristics:

1. Crime rates are low enough so that most people consider it safe to walk on the streets at any time during the day and some of the time at night.
2. Housing and other structures are maintained in good physical condition.
3. Neighborhood schools are considered adequate or more than adequate by most local residents.

4. Streets are reasonably free from trash, abandoned automobiles, and other debris, and local public services are considered adequate by most residents.
5. The area is reasonably convenient to normal urban facilities (such as shopping, employment centers, and churches) and is served by public transportation to a degree enabling its residents to accomplish their major movement goals. (In many suburban areas, this does not require any public transportation.)
6. Most people who live in the area or are considering living there believe that the above conditions are likely to persist for an indefinite period—at least for five years.

Neighborhoods can be considered viable for households without children if they exhibit all the above traits except adequate schools.

The best practical way to determine whether a neighborhood is viable is to examine behavior in the market for its housing. Most people who have a meaningful choice among many places to live will not move into a neighborhood they think lacks any of the above characteristics. For this reason, a neighborhood can be considered viable if more than half of the households moving into it during the most recent year are affluent enough to enjoy a choice among many different residential areas—including some that clearly exhibit the above traits.

WHY MOST AREAS OF CONCENTRATED POVERTY ARE NOT VIABLE

Many studies of conditions in crisis ghettos confirm that most areas of concentrated poverty are not viable. Such studies range from dramatic autobiographies like *Manchild in the Promised Land* to massive factual reports like that of the National Advisory Commission on Civil Disorders. Again and again the point is made that large numbers of urban poor people living together in our society usually do not constitute a healthy environment for normal life.

Why is this true? The answer can best be understood by more closely examining the dynamics of spatially concentrated poverty. As explained in chapter 1, poor people begin to cluster together in the older parts of large cities because the obsolete and deteriorated housing there is relatively inexpensive. Moreover, construction of *new* inexpensive housing in more peripheral neighborhoods is prevented by rigorous enforcement of high-quality building codes. The resulting spatial concentration of poverty is reinforced for many minority groups by racial and ethnic segregation.

The concentration of poverty thus generated contains two different types of poor households: the mainstream poor and the left-out poor (defined in chapter 4).[1] Since both share the basic values and aspirations of middle-class Americans, both want to escape from poverty. The mainstream poor—except for the elderly—believe they are capable of escaping soon. Their behavior is almost the same as middle-class behavior, except they lack money. The left-out poor, who no longer believe they can escape from poverty in the foreseeable future, may shift to adaptive behavior that differs from middle-class behavior and often creates negative spillover effects upon surrounding households. As sociologist Kenneth Clark has pointed out, " 'Cashing in' and the 'hustle' reflect the belief that one cannot make a living through socially acceptable vocations." [2] Robert Weaver, the first Secretary of Housing and Urban Development, has also linked negative behavior patterns with feelings of being left out:

> It is . . . unrealistic . . . to expect most of those who are denied middle-class rewards to strive for what experience has demonstrated to be unobtainable to them. . . . The social pathology of slums and blighted areas will persist as long as elements in our population are relegated to what seems to their members as an institutional submerged status.[3]

Weaver also indicated that the behavior of certain types of households in poverty areas can create negative spillover effects:

> Certain elements now concentrated in the slums . . . present clear and well-defined problems. They include the confirmed middle-age winos, the established prostitutes, the overt homosexuals, the hardened criminals, and the like, who either resist rehabilitation or require long-term assistance of a most intensive type. They are multi-ethnic and constitute the real "hard core." In addition, the classical problem families which usually evidence some form of anti-social behavior are well-represented among slum residents.[4]

The emergence of these negative spillover effects causes many middle-income households remaining in areas of concentrated poverty to move elsewhere and encourages many mainstream poor to leave as soon as they raise their incomes. The departure of these more affluent households—and the unwillingness of others like them to move in—create an even greater concentration of poor people in the area. This may be aggravated if the city is experiencing large-scale low-income in-migration. Soon the area's environment becomes dominated by negative spillover effects from the behavior of a minority of left-out poor households.

It should be re-emphasized that only a small fraction of low-income households in concentrated poverty areas exhibit these negative behavior patterns. Nevertheless, widespread poverty reduces normal powers of resistance to such behavior, and it does not take many households generating negative behavior to create an environment that nearly all Americans would regard as highly undesirable. The nature of that environment was described in chapters 1, 2, and 4.

Many private firms that provide jobs for local residents soon move out of concentrated poverty areas to escape vandalism and increasing difficulties in recruiting a satisfactory labor force. Retail firms serving the area decrease in number as total spending falls, further cutting available jobs. And a series of exploitative institutions arises to prey upon the poor, ranging from high-cost-credit appliance stores and unscrupulous landlords to dope pushers and numbers operators. The residents' awareness of their relatively impoverished and exploited condition is heightened by constant contrasts between their area and "normal America" as depicted on television—which even the poorest Americans watch daily. The feelings of hopelessness typical of the left-out poor are thus reinforced. Some mainstream poor become affected by those feelings, too, and shift to the left-out poor category.

Thus a vicious circle of deepening poverty and despair is generated in many older urban areas. Because the lack of income flowing into such areas makes it impossible to pay for proper maintenance of housing and other physical structures regardless of who owns them, these structures become ever more deteriorated and less desirable. Poor households have higher rates of both physical and mental illness than other income groups, so the incidence of these pathologies rises. Moreover, because the poorest people are usually the least organized and the least capable of mobilizing their own resources, they are less successful in gaining assistance through political channels than residents of more affluent areas.

Once this self-perpetuating process of impoverishment gets underway, it is extremely difficult to reverse. Few households or business firms affluent enough to have a choice of locations are willing to move into such an area and many already there move out. Yet without them, the area cannot become economically self-sustaining enough to start rising out of poverty. Also, the more difficult it becomes for local residents to escape poverty, the stronger their feelings of being left out of society—and the less motivation many have to adopt middle-class behavior patterns.

I recognize that the above explanation contains many unproven theories. One example is Lee Rainwater's theory that certain "lower-class" behavior patterns are adaptations to feeling left out of "mainstream" society. Nevertheless, there is overwhelming evidence that most Americans—including most residents of concentrated poverty areas—consider the environment prevailing in such areas to be highly undesirable. The conclusion that concentrated poverty *somehow* generates non-viable environments is all that is necessary to support the major contentions of this book.

DEGREES OF POVERTY CONCENTRATION

What percentage of a neighborhood's residents must be poor for it to be an area of "concentrated poverty"? Little research has been done on either the concept of neighborhood viability or its relation to other characteristics. However, the following data provide some interim insights.

In the nation as a whole, about 13 percent of the population was "poor" in 1970.[5] (At that time, any four-person household with an annual income of under $3,944 was considered poor. Analogous incomes applied to households of other sizes.) Within central cities, about 10.9 percent of all families and 29.5 percent of all unrelated individuals were poor. Data for neighborhoods of elementary school attendance area size are not readily available, but figures for somewhat larger poverty areas have been obtained from Chicago's Model Cities Program. Data for eight areas containing "concentrated poverty" as measured by a variety of other indicators are set forth in table 4.

The proportion of households in these areas with total 1969 incomes below $3,000 (somewhat lower than the official poverty level for a four-person household) ranged from 13.0 to 45.2 percent. The proportion of households with 1969 incomes below $5,000 (close to the official poverty level for larger households) ranged from 30.4 to 68.3 percent. Area E, which has the highest percentages in both categories, contains an enormous amount of public housing. Omitting that area, it is reasonable to conclude that *a neighborhood can be considered too poor to be viable even when far less than half of its occupants have incomes below the official poverty line.* That is about all that can now be said about this relationship.

Some neighborhoods may have a low enough percentage of poor households to be viable and yet not be "dominated" by middle-income or middle-class characteristics. We cannot determine this until more precise definitions of viability and

Table 4
Proportions of Low-Income Households
in Areas of Concentrated Poverty

Chicago Model Cities Area	*Percentage of Households with Total 1969 Pre-Tax Incomes of:*		
	Under $3,000	$3,000 to $4,999	Under $5,000
A	28.5	14.1	42.6
B	13.0	25.0	38.0
C	13.0	17.4	30.4
D	15.9	22.5	38.4
E	45.2	23.1	68.3
F	27.2	21.8	49.0
G	23.4	28.0	51.4
H	21.8	21.6	43.4

SOURCE: Based upon a 2 percent random sample of households in each area surveyed for the Chicago Model Cities Agency. Results obtained from unpublished memoranda for the Chicago Model Cities Agency.

middle-class dominance have been tested empirically. However, in the remainder of this analysis, I will assume that when the percentage of poor households in any neighborhood falls low enough so it is considered viable by the local housing market, that area is dominated by middle-class traits. This contention is reinforced by my belief that most households affluent enough to enjoy a choice among many residential areas (and whose continued entry is the best evidence of viability) deliberately seek out areas where middle-class traits are dominant, for reasons discussed below.

WHY THE MIDDLE CLASS WANTS NEIGHBORHOOD DOMINANCE

Most middle- and upper-income households want to live where they are personally safe, where their homes are safe and at least maintain initial economic values, and where their children are exposed to cultural value-reinforcing experiences (mainly with children from other middle-income households).

These conditions create neighborhood viability for them. None would be seriously weakened by the presence of some low- and moderate-income households in the area. Hence middle- and upper-income households can attain their basic residential objectives through *dominance* of their neighborhoods and do not require *total exclusion* of low- and moderate-income households. This conclusion is consistent with both numerous opinion polls and actual neighborhood experience.

As noted above, it is not clear what percentage of a neighborhood can consist of low- and moderate-income households without disrupting middle-class dominance. But I presume it is well under 50 percent and is further limited by two criteria: there must be no perceptible negative change in dominant behavior patterns (such as the emergence of street gangs); and this percentage must be low enough—and rising slowly enough—so that middle- and upper-income households do not believe the neighborhood will soon lose its middle-class dominance.

WHY LOW- AND MODERATE-INCOME HOUSEHOLDS NEED MIDDLE-CLASS NEIGHBORHOOD DOMINANCE

Many low- and moderate-income households also need to live in neighborhoods where middle-class influences are dominant in order to achieve their own residential objectives. The mainstream poor, who share both middle-class values and middle-class behavior patterns, would have this orientation reinforced. Since their aspirations cannot be satisfied without living in a middle-class milieu, even though they now lack the money to do so, economic integration would surely have beneficial effects for them.

But what about the left-out poor? Some of this group have adapted themselves to economic failure so fully that they do not feel any positive desire to live in a middle-class milieu. Nevertheless, most certainly have a strong desire to escape from the negative conditions in areas of concentrated poverty. This "escape" would be a benefit even if they were not "upgraded" by the move. Perhaps some upgrading effects would result from the provision of the more visible models of success and more accessible opportunities for achieving it themselves that a predominantly middle-class milieu would provide. There is some evidence supporting this conclusion regarding children in public schools, as discussed earlier.[6] But there is not much other evidence about the extent to which such an upgrading effect would occur for the left-out poor. In theory, greater exposure to middle-class life might produce certain more healthful mores and behavior than they would have developed in concentrated poverty areas. However, the contrast between middle-class consumption standards and what poorer households could afford might be humiliating and discouraging to many low-income residents. Moreover, if the areas concerned did not provide the specific social services that many poor households need (such as family counseling and free health clinics), they might suffer some deprivations worse than in poverty areas.

Thus, merely mixing some left-out poor households with middle-income households in a neighborhood dominated by the latter would not necessarily produce any net "positive uplift" upon the former. The actual effects would be greatly influenced by the attitudes and behavior of the area's middle-income residents. If they remained highly class-conscious and failed to adapt their behavior to be more hospitable to people with less money, they might prevent any "positive uplift." For example, local high school socializing might involve expensive dances and proms. If no changes were made to permit students with little money to participate on a roughly equal basis, then low-income young people might become frustrated and hostile toward middle-class values.

Nevertheless, even where "positive uplift" effects upon the left-out poor were absent, low- and moderate-income households would still benefit from living in middle-class dominated neighborhoods because they would be removed from the detrimental environment of concentrated poverty areas. Moreover, the mainstream poor would be in the milieu they prefer.

It is probably necessary for a significant number of low- and moderate-income households to reside in a dominantly middle-class area to produce the best results. If only a few poor households lived in a neighborhood containing 5,000 people, they might feel isolated. Furthermore, their votes would not be important enough to pressure local government to provide them with services tailored to their needs. But if, say, 500 to 1,000 people in that area were in low- and moderate-income households, they would not feel isolated and could exert significant political pressure. Middle-income residents would be more aware of their existence and perhaps more willing to shift previous behavior patterns to help meet their needs.

The Charge of "Middle-Class Chauvinism"

The preceding analysis indicates that middle-class neighborhood dominance benefits *both* most middle- and upper-income households and many (perhaps most) low- and moderate-income households. In contrast, concentration of poverty injures almost all households where it occurs. Therefore, it appears that public policies should be aimed at encouraging middle-class dominance and eliminating poverty concentrations wherever possible.

This conclusion may seem a form of cultural chauvinism to those who believe all behavior patterns and life styles deserve equal public-policy treatment. I do not agree. The evidence is conclusive that certain life styles produce destructive results that society is justified in opposing in its own self-defense. For example, becoming a drug addict is not just one morally neutral choice among possible consumption patterns. Drug addicts typically engage in burglary, robbery, prostitution, and other destructive acts in order to support their expensive habits. Similarly, it is socially irresponsible to father several children by different mothers and then refuse to contribute to the financial or moral support of the mothers or the children. Children reared without fathers are more prone to neuroses and more likely to engage in various kinds of antisocial behavior than those reared by both parents. This is most harmful to the children themselves, but it is also costly to others.

Middle-class mores and behavior are certainly far from

perfect. We should neither condone nor encourage their failings—such as tendencies toward racism and hostility toward harmless deviant behavior. Yet concerning the social linkages described in chapter 6, I believe neighborhood dominance by middle-class behavior patterns is normally preferable to prevalence of the destructive behavior patterns typical in areas of concentrated poverty. On the other hand, attributing such destructive behavior patterns to a majority of low-income households is indeed "middle-class chauvinism," since only a small minority exhibit destructive behavior.

Neighborhood Racial Dominance

Most American white middle-class households want to maintain *racial* dominance in their own neighborhoods as well as *economic class* dominance. In this case, "dominance" means a preponderance of whites in an area and in its institutions.[7]

Clearly, race and color have no necessary linkage with the kinds of social, cultural, economic, or religious characteristics and values that have a true functional impact upon adults and children. Yet a majority of middle-class white Americans still perceive race and color as relevant to the kind of neighborhood homogeneity they desire. In deciding whether a particular neighborhood or school exhibits an environment in which "their own" traits are and will remain dominant, they consider blacks and other minority-group members as belonging to "other" groups. However demeaning this unjustified behavior may be to minority-group members, it must be recognized as real if we are to understand why residential segregation by race has persisted so strongly in the United States and what conditions are necessary to create viable racial integration. The expansion of black residential areas has led to massive transition from white to black occupancy mainly because there has been no legal mechanism that could assure the whites in any area that they would remain in the majority after blacks began to enter.

Once blacks begin entering an all-white neighborhood near a racial ghetto, most whites become convinced the area will eventually become all black, because this has happened so often before. Hence it is difficult to persuade whites not now living there to move into vacancies arising through normal housing turnover. They are willing to move only where whites seem likely to remain the dominant majority. So almost all vacancies are occupied by blacks, and the neighborhood inexorably shifts toward a heavy black majority. Once this happens, the remaining whites also try to leave.

As a result, whites who would be quite satisfied to live in an integrated neighborhood *as members of the majority* are never given an opportunity to do so. Instead, for reasons beyond the control of each individual, they are forced to choose between complete racial segregation and living in areas heavily dominated by members of what they consider "another group." Given their values, they choose the former.

Under these conditions, achieving stable racially integrated neighborhoods requires four ingredients now difficult to produce. The first is the ability to convince whites that their majority status will persist in mixed areas in spite of past experience to the contrary. This in turn requires the second ingredient: a workable mechanism ensuring that whites will remain in a majority—such as some type of quota system— that is both legal and credible. The third ingredient consists of minority-group members willing to reside in a predominantly white neighborhood. And the last is some means of persuading whites not actually living in the mixed area to move in from elsewhere so as to maintain its racial balance as vacancies occur. This requires achievement of the first two ingredients.

The use of quotas or other explicit "racial balancing" mechanisms is deplored by many who theoretically support racial integration. During the 1972 presidential campaign it was attacked by an especially broad spectrum of critics, including candidates of both parties. Nevertheless, almost all racially integrated neighborhoods and housing developments that have remained integrated for very long have used deliberate management to achieve certain numerical targets as to the proportion of minority-group occupants. In other words, they used quotas. In my opinion, stable racial integration under present conditions absolutely requires such racial

discrimination. Completely "color blind" policies quickly lead
to racial segregation if the area or development concerned is
close to a large and expanding concentration of minority-
group members. Failure to use some recognized racial balancing mechanism causes whites to believe the area will soon
become predominantly black once *any* blacks enter. Then
whites rapidly withdraw, leaving the area segregated.

The need for explicit racial discrimination to achieve stable
racial integration has already been legally recognized in court
decisions concerning both public schools and the location of
public housing. There is an exactly analogous need for specific
"economic balancing" mechanisms to achieve stable economic
integration, as discussed further in chapter 10.

Many liberals have attacked advocacy of explicit racial
balance targets on the grounds that they cannot work or will
be misused or will deprive qualified non-minority-group
individuals of their rights. However, all social arrangements
are imperfect and therefore involve some degree of injustice;
the question is which form of injustice is least undesirable in
light of all costs and benefits. I believe achieving some degree
of integration—both economic and racial—is far better than
allowing our society to become almost totally segregated
simply because we were unwilling to adopt specific numerical
targets for mixtures of people. Every experienced businessman,
union leader, and government official knows that planning of
any kind—whether aimed at profits or at public welfare—is
far more effective when linked to specific numerical targets
than when dependent only on vague general exhortations. As
Vernon E. Jordan, Jr., of the Urban League put it concerning
employment programs:

> Anyone from the man with a shovel to the men
> contending for the White House knows that without some
> sort of effective numerical guidelines, no affirmative
> action hiring plan can work. Reliance on "Good faith
> efforts" is doomed to failure. The history of past and
> present discrimination is ample proof of that.[8]

ECONOMIC AND RACIAL NEIGHBORHOOD DOMINANCE COMPARED

There is one profound difference between white middle-class desires for racial and economic class neighborhood dominance. Poverty can and does have truly functional relations to behavior patterns that are relevant to the quality of neighborhood life. But race and color do not. Hence I believe the middle-class desire for *racial* dominance will gradually disappear in the minds of many (but not all) white Americans. This will occur as more and more whites discover that minority-group individuals with the same incomes as their own share the same values and behavior patterns. Many white middle-class Americans may then be willing to live in racially integrated—but economically homogeneous—neighborhoods with black majorities, if a significant number of other whites live there too. They will also send their children to schools where black children are in a majority, if those schools are overwhelmingly middle-class in student composition.

In contrast, I doubt that most middle-class Americans—white or black—will alter their desire for neighborhood economic class dominance as long as a significant fraction of the poor exhibit behavior patterns different from those prevalent in middle-class areas. Therefore, in the long run, I expect economic class discrimination to be more persistent in American residential neighborhoods than racial discrimination, even though the latter has been stronger up to now. This does not mean that neighborhoods predominantly occupied by members of one ethnic group (such as blacks or Jews or Puerto Ricans) will soon disappear. Such areas will remain part of American urban life for a long time, because many members of ethnic groups prefer living in areas where their "own" group is locally dominant. However, I believe residential discrimination aimed at *excluding* members of ethnic minorities is likely to fade out long before discrimination aimed at excluding the poor. In fact, the latter will remain strong until society adopts specific policies to counteract it, such as those proposed by this book.

10 Achieving Economically Balanced Population

A key strategic concept in opening up the suburbs is attaining economically balanced population at different geographic scales. The term *balanced population* refers to that mixture of social groups which best serves a specific objective. The following four objectives of population mixture are necessary to achieving the various benefits of opening up the suburbs described in chapter 4:

1. Convenient access to suburban jobs for low- and moderate-income households
2. Attendance at economically integrated public schools by children from such households
3. Daily personal interaction between members of such households and members of middle- and upper-income households nearby
4. Opportunities for low and moderate-income households to escape the disadvantages inherent in large concentrations of poverty

Past failure to distinguish among these objectives has caused confusion about how suburban economic integration might be achieved and has generated much unnecessary opposition to it. It is especially crucial to recognize that each objective requires a different geographic scale of suburban economic integration.

ACCESS TO JOBS

The largest scale is related to providing decent housing for low- and moderate-income households within convenient commuting range of suburban jobs. There are many ways to define the population balance needed to attain this objective, only one of which is described here to illustrate the basic principles involved.

Each metropolitan area could be divided into several "commuting zones" for planning purposes. Two conditions would be necessary to achieve population balance in any zone. First, the number, types, and price ranges of the housing located within a zone should be adequate to provide a suitable housing unit for everyone who works within that zone. Second, all the housing within a zone should be within some specified rush-hour commuting time by public transportation from all the jobs in the zone. (I have used 30 minutes in this analysis because it is slightly above the national median commuting time.)[1] If both these conditions existed, anyone working within any commuting zone would be able to find a decent home suitable to his income and family size located within convenient commuting time from his job.

What geographic scale of residential economic integration would this approach require? To be conservative, I assume that the average commuter using public transportation (if there is any) could move at 10 miles per hour. If a typical commuting zone were a square with a diagonal 5 miles long, then movement from one corner to the farthest point within the zone (the opposite corner) would take 30 minutes. The total area of this typical zone would be 12.5 square miles. Zones on the edge of the metropolitan area might be even larger, since lower congestion would allow longer commutes in 30 minutes. Thus, commuting zones could contain relatively large populations. For example, Berkeley, California had a 1970 population of 117,000 in 10.6 square miles. By the definition described above, all of Berkeley could be considered a single commuting zone.

Providing a wide range of housing types and price levels within such a large zone would not necessarily require low- and moderate-income households to live very close to, or highly intermixed with, middle- and upper-income households. Assume, for instance, that members of low- and moderate-income households containing 30,000 people hold 30 percent of all the jobs in Berkeley. As long as they all lived in decent housing *somewhere* within Berkeley, there would be an economically balanced population *insofar as the job convenience objective was concerned.* All 30,000 might even live in one huge neighborhood, totally separated from all the middle- and upper-income households in the community.

Nevertheless, achievement of the job convenience objective would require major changes in the existing spatial distribution of housing in relation to income groups. In most American metropolitan areas, the proportion of low-income households in total population is lower the greater the distance of any subarea from the central business district. However, the proportion of low-income *jobs* does not fall as rapidly as the proportion of low-income *housing* as distance from downtown increases. Consequently, many low-income workers commute from close-in homes to jobs farther out, and many high-income workers do the opposite. So there is probably a "shortage" of low- and moderate-income housing in commuting zones on the fringes of large metropolitan areas compared to the amount of such housing required to achieve population balance.[2] Conversely, in most central-city commuting zones, "surpluses" of such housing are likely to be found.

Since this particular concept of how to achieve population balance has not been tested empirically, public policy should not yet become committed to it or to any other specific formula for balancing housing and jobs. First we need to conduct tests to determine the practical implications of various standards. Nevertheless, we should eventually adopt some official *population balance target* for housing in each part of every metropolitan area in America to improve suburban job accessibility for low- and moderate-income households.

There are four main theoretical disadvantages of this approach. First, experience proves there will always be "cross-commuting" among zones. Many people working in any given commuting zone will live outside its boundaries even if suitable housing is available within that zone, and many residents of each zone will work somewhere else, even if they could move closer to their jobs. Yet it is still desirable to strive for the kind of economic balance between jobs and housing described above. If it existed, the normal turnover in housing markets would provide excellent opportunities for households of every income to live closer to their jobs *if they wanted to*. Unquestionably, many would do so. Consequently, the average amount of commuting would probably decline, and low- and moderate-income households would suffer less unemployment in the long run.

A second problem with this approach is that each central business district would distort the economic balance everywhere in its metropolitan area. Many jobs are concentrated in these centers, but jobholders live scattered widely throughout the metropolitan area. As a result, there would be an "automatic" imbalance between jobs and housing in all parts of the area. However, this condition could easily be taken into account by making slight adjustments in defining the desired balance in each zone.

A third difficulty in applying this approach is that no appropriate political or legal authority exists either to conduct or to implement such planning. This deficiency will be discussed in chapters 12 and 14.

The final disadvantage of economic mixture at this scale is that it would not necessarily prevent the concentration of large numbers of low-income households. Such households might still be plagued by many of the disadvantages of central-city crisis ghettos if they lived in large suburban clusters of concentrated poverty. Nevertheless, a series of suburban "mini-ghettos" would have several advantages over the single massive crisis ghetto now found in many large metropolitan areas. "Mini-ghetto" residents would have more convenient access to expanding suburban job opportunities. Closer proximity of non-poor suburbanites to the problems of concentrated poverty might cause them to take more effective action against those problems. And various types of interaction with surrounding non-poor residents that are hopelessly difficult to arrange when 200,000 poor people are clustered together are at least conceivable when, say, 30,000 are clustered together— and much more so at still smaller scales.

Because of the above factors, it would be unrealistic to strive for a *precise* balance between housing and jobs in each commuting zone. Our economy is too dynamic and its decision-making is too decentralized. Nevertheless, setting some rough target combination of jobs and housing for each part of each metropolitan area would provide far more useful guidance to public policy-makers than now exists.

INTEGRATION OF SCHOOLS

The second type of population balance is that required to provide opportunities for children from low- and moderate-income households to attend schools where children from middle- and upper-income households predominate. This would improve the education received by the children from low- and moderate-income households and broaden the educational and democratic experience of the children from both groups.

As already noted, the present relationship between where children live and what school they attend is usually governed by the "neighborhood school principle." Insofar as practical, attendance area boundaries for each school are drawn so that each child attends the school nearest his or her residence.[3] If we assume that the average urban elementary school contains about 750 students, then the neighborhood that school serves contains around 5,000 persons. Attaining economic integration at the elementary school level—while retaining middle-class dominance in each school—means creating a residential pattern in which from 10 to 20 percent of the households in each 5,000-person elementary school attendance area have low and moderate incomes. The average gross population density in most suburban areas is less than 5,000 persons per square mile, so this type of population balance would have to occur in areas of 640 acres or less. Thus the population balance needed for economically integrated elementary schools requires residential mixture of the poor and non-poor at a much smaller geographic scale than that required to provide adequate job accessibility.

Nevertheless, considerable spatial separation of these two groups could still occur under this type of population balance.

If this "typical" suburban attendance area contained a total of 640 acres, about one-half—or 320 acres—would be in net residential use. Relatively low-cost single-family homes might attain a net residential density of about 25 persons per acre. Therefore, a single neighborhood containing 40 acres net could accommodate 1,000 low- and moderate-income residents, who would constitute 20 percent of a school attendance area containing 5,000 residents. If they lived in apartments or townhouses at a net residential density of 15 units per acre, they could be spatially separated in an even smaller area— about 23 acres. The remaining 297 net residential acres could be occupied by 4,000 middle- and upper-income residents. I am not necessarily advocating such spatial separation of low- and moderate-income households within economically integrated school attendance areas. Rather, I am pointing out the degree of spatial mixture *required* to achieve each basic objective of suburban economic integration.

Economic integration of suburban elementary schools could be attained with even greater spatial separation of these groups if the neighborhood school principle were removed as a constraint. For example, consider a school district containing five square miles, with 5,000 residents within each square mile and one elementary school at the center of each square mile. If the district bused some students, then all 5,000 of the low- and moderate-income residents in the entire district could *live* within a single square mile; while their children were comprising 20 percent of the attendance at each school. This strategy does not require every student to ride a bus. The percentage of students bused could vary anywhere from zero to 50, depending upon exactly where the various economic groups and schools were located. In view of current resistance to busing children to achieve socioeconomic objectives, however, it may not be feasible to use this approach in many areas.

In general, economic integration of schools can be accomplished either by encouraging more low- and moderate-income households to move into attendance areas where few children from such households now attend school or by changing existing attendance area boundaries. The housing tactic should be emphasized where *new* residential development is occurring or where the existing housing stock is suitable for occupancy by low- and moderate-income households aided by subsidies. The boundary-changing tactic should be emphasized where many low- and moderate-income households already reside in or near suburban school districts but attend schools with few middle- and upper-income children. Unless busing is feasible, this type of population balance is probably not attainable in attendance areas that are fully built up with very costly housing and are also far from vacant land and from existing housing suitable for low- and moderate-income occupancy. Therefore, population balance in regard to elementary schools should not be considered quite as universal an objective of public policy as the type required for suburban job accessibility.[4]

Achieving the population balance required for economic integration of *high schools* could be a more nearly universal policy objective. If the average suburban public high school contains 2,000 students, it serves a total population of about 30,000.[5] It would surely be easier to locate housing for low- and moderate-income households, or redraw attendance area boundaries, to obtain an appropriate population balance in such a relatively large area than within each elementary school attendance area.

DAILY PERSONAL INTERACTION AMONG HOUSEHOLDS

Daily personal interactions between low- and moderate-income households and more affluent households are most likely to occur if these households are intermixed at a very small scale—almost within every block. Children, especially very young ones, tend to play daily only with others living within a few houses at most. The play patterns of children strongly influence the social interactions of parents, especially in suburbs. Therefore, achieving habitual daily interaction across economic group lines would require thorough scatteration of individual low- and moderate-income households throughout areas occupied mainly by middle- and high-income households. Wherever this occurred, middle- and upper-income households would have to be convinced that low- and moderate-income households were not going to become locally dominant, as explained earlier. Also, low- and moderate-income households probably should not reside in dwelling units obviously less expensive than those of their neighbors. This might adversely affect resale values of surrounding homes unless such intermixture were required everywhere else, too; and it might "brand" less affluent households and thereby reduce their self-respect and sense of confidence and dignity. The undesirability of using obviously less expensive units has not yet been fully tested in practice, however.

Achieving economic intermixture will be much more difficult at this small geographic scale than at the two previously discussed scales. Many builders now create sizable clusters of new homes with about the same price, design, and basic character. Mixing in lower income households at a "fine grain" would require one of two changes in existing practices. One would be providing large subsidies per household to maintain homogeneity of housing unit quality. The second would be requiring almost all residential developers to scatter low- and moderate-income units in every block within their new developments.

It is questionable whether many low- and moderate-income households actually want to live in such relative isolation from each other amid more affluent neighbors. Many would probably prefer living in clusters with other low- and moderate-income households. If so, what size should such clusters be in order to both give their members a sense of identity and cohesion with others like themselves and allow meaningful daily interaction with more affluent households? In the "new city" of Columbia, Maryland, clusters of about sixty units of such housing appear to work out well. But not enough experience has been accumulated to answer this question with much confidence. We need much more experimentation with different scales of economic group intermixture in actual neighborhoods—both new and existing—before setting any specific standards.

The difficulties associated with achieving this kind of

population balance make it the type least attainable in the near future. Public policy should therefore probably seek to establish population balance at this scale in only a relatively small number of suburban neighborhoods in each metropolitan area in the near future. Yet it is vital not to abandon this type of population balance as a long-range objective. The personal interaction possible only at this scale may ultimately be our best hope to assist many multiproblem low- and moderate-income households.

AVOIDING THE NEGATIVE EFFECTS OF CONCENTRATED POVERTY

Another vital question about the proper scale for economic integration is: how small must clusters of mainly low- and moderate-income households be to avoid the negative effects of concentrated poverty? Again, no one has sufficient experience to answer this question reliably, but I believe the answer depends in part upon the types of low- and moderate-income households concerned. When most multiproblem families were kept out of public housing, even large-scale public housing projects were considered highly desirable by low-income households. Once these projects began to accept many multiproblem families, their desirability declined as crime rates, vandalism, and other negative conditions multiplied.

This raises the touchy issue of qualitative screening of those low- and moderate-income households who will reside in mainly middle- and upper-income areas. Should officials try to screen out families with multiple problems or destructive tendencies? Doing so would greatly improve the acceptability of dispersing low- and moderate-income households in the eyes of present suburbanites. On the other hand, it would increase the concentration of multiproblem households left behind in crisis ghettos, and it would deny opportunities for upgrading to many of those who need them most. Furthermore, it would require public officials to make highly subjective judgments about individual households.

Nevertheless, failure to select stable households to begin the movement into mainly middle- and upper-income neighborhoods could easily be fatal to this strategy. Experience with many groups initially suspicious of each other indicates that members of each group exaggerate the extent of undesirable behavior carried out by the other. For example, studies of the interaction of big-city police and low-income blacks show that a few truly reprehensible actions on each side are so widely discussed that they are taken as much more representative than they really are. This false perception reinforces the hostility that generated it in the first place—and thereby increases the probability that real conflicts will occur. Such self-fulfilling prophecy could easily be the result of mixing poor and non-poor households in suburban areas. This could generate such powerful middle-class hostility to continuation of economic integration that it would be hastily abandoned. To avoid that outcome, those responsible for administering economic integration policies should, at least in the beginning, keep the fraction of multiproblem families involved very low.

MECHANISMS TO CREATE AND MAINTAIN POPULATION BALANCE

Discussing population balance is a vain exercise unless specific mechanisms are available to achieve it. I believe the following would work:

1. *Residential density controls.* In some suburbs, prevailing quality standards make single-family housing too costly for low- and moderate-income households—even when subsidized. By controlling the percentage of the community zoned for multifamily units, planning authorities could both create opportunities for low- and moderate-income households to live there and limit the proportion of such households in the area.

2. *Housing subsidy allocations.* Low- and moderate-income households cannot live in most suburbs without direct federal housing subsidies. Authorities seeking population balance could be given significant influence over the geographic allocation of such subsidies in each metropolitan area.

3. *Planned unit development zoning.* Any community can establish zoning rules that treat large developments as special entities and impose certain overall requirements on them. One

such requirement could be providing a certain minimum fraction of all housing units for low- and moderate-income households.

4. *Required "economic balance targets" for all new development over some minimum size.* All developers creating more than a specific number of units in any project (say, twenty-five units) could be required to allocate a minimum share (say, from 10 to 20 percent) to initial occupancy by low- and moderate-income households. Any such requirement would have to be accompanied by sufficient federal housing subsidy funding to make it feasible.

The above mechanisms provide workable means of establishing and maintaining population balance in a given area. By carefully orchestrating them, public officials could conceivably influence the nature and location of new residential development and the allocation of subsidies to older existing housing so as to attain population balance at all four previously described scales in at least some parts of each metropolitan area.

Except in areas with metropolitan governments, no one now has the authority to use such mechanisms throughout enough of any metropolitan area to achieve or maintain effective population balance. Few officials have the skill and sophistication to use these mechanisms so as to achieve population balance simultaneously at the four scales described above. Furthermore, in recent years most citizens have become skeptical about government officials' ability to deal effectively with *any* social problems. Therefore my assertion that they can use the above mechanisms to achieve population balance will be regarded as naïve optimism by many.

However, we are already effectively using some of these same mechanisms to exclude almost all low- and moderate-income households from new-growth portions of suburbia and to concentrate them in the oldest parts of large central cities and some suburbs. These results demonstrate how effectively public officials can pursue those objectives they truly value. The choice facing us is not whether to use the above mechanisms but what objectives to pursue in using them.

Yet orchestrating all these mechanisms to attain population balance concerning all four of the above objectives simultaneously may be an unrealistic goal at present. Local government structures are now too fragmented to permit achieving such multilevel population balance, especially when many local officials want to exclude the poor altogether. In that case, I advocate pursuing the following more modest objectives:

1. Putting top priority initially upon achieving population balance concerning the job accessibility objective in as many portions of as many metropolitan areas as possible

2. Using a decentralized decision strategy that leaves most of the initiative for choosing suburban low- and moderate-income housing locations with private builders and developers. This strategy is described in chapter 12.

11 Why Improving the Inner City
Requires Opening Up the Suburbs

Countless urban experts and political leaders have deplored the spreading crisis ghetto conditions in many large cities. However, few recognize that these conditions are indissolubly linked to what is happening in the outlying parts of the same metropolitan areas, as described in chapter 1. Under present conditions, continued rapid expansion of the nation's housing supply—which is favored by most political leaders—will accelerate the housing abandonment and spreading inner-city decay they decry. Moreover, *no strategies for improving crisis ghetto conditions will work in the long run without opening up the suburbs.*

In fact, as mentioned in chapter 4, improving those conditions is one of the potential benefits of opening up the suburbs. Both ghetto improvement and opening up the suburbs should be part of any overall urban strategy for America. Before setting forth what I believe should be the key principles of such a strategy in chapter 12, I will try to demonstrate in this chapter why these two courses of action are so inextricably related—and thus why it is fundamentally inconsistent to advocate improving the nation's crisis ghettos and at the same time to oppose opening up the suburbs.

LINKAGES BETWEEN NEW SUBURBS AND CRISIS GHETTOS

Every brand-new occupied suburban housing unit contains a household that would be living somewhere else if that unit had not been built. Most such households have left other units in the same metropolitan area. The people who move into those existing units, in turn, leave other units available. The average chain of moves thus created by each newly built unit involves from 2.0 to 3.5 households. Moreover, one 1965 study indicated that 9.4 percent of all the households induced to move as a result of new construction had incomes below the poverty level.[1]

This is how the trickle-down process works. The more new, relatively high-cost housing built in new-growth neighborhoods, the more units elsewhere in the existing stock become available for households who cannot afford brand-new units. True, new housing construction may be offset by rising natural increase in the local population, net in-migration, demolitions and other removals from the existing stock, or sufficient affluence for existing households to separate into several parts. But every net increase in a metropolitan area's housing supply relative to its housing demand tends to "loosen" its entire housing market—not just where new construction is occurring. In addition, available vacancies eventually become concentrated in the oldest and worst housing. The owners of better quality units keep adjusting their rents and prices to attract occupants. It is true that ethnic segregation impedes unrestricted movement of many economically capable households upward through the existing inventory. Yet large net housing supply increases in predominantly white areas soon affect conditions in nearby mainly nonwhite areas too. This occurs primarily through the process of massive ethnic transition in neighborhoods on the edges of racial ghettos. When whites in those areas have many alternative places to live, they depart faster after minority-group members begin entering.

Consequently, any significant surplus of total housing supply in relation to total demand within a metropolitan area accelerates the entire trickle-down process. It allows many households at all income levels to improve their housing conditions. Naturally, those in the worst housing have the greatest desire to do so; hence many residents of crisis ghettos move out of the oldest, most deteriorated units in the least secure neighborhoods. If no new wave of immigrants enters the city, this leads to abandonment of these units. Thus, *massive construction of new housing for people at the upper end of the income distribution is one of the necessary conditions for large-scale housing abandonment at the lower end.* (Certain other conditions are also necessary for abandonment, but they are too complex to discuss here.)[2]

Abandonment usually indicates that many low-income households are moving into adjacent neighborhoods. If the number of such households is large, those neighborhoods soon become areas of concentrated poverty too. They are then dominated by the same adverse conditions prevalent in the areas being abandoned. Thus the spreading of crisis ghetto conditions in older inner-city areas is made possible—even encouraged—whenever there is enough *net* new housing construction within the metropolitan area to increase area-wide vacancy significantly.

Rapidly spreading neighborhood deterioration caused by movement of poor households out of the worst crisis ghettos began long before either housing abandonment or rising overall vacancy. It was first stimulated by massive immigration from abroad in the nineteenth century. Such immigration slowed down in the 1920s and 1930s but was replaced by large-scale influxes of blacks, Puerto Ricans, and Mexican Americans during and after World War II. Early urban renewal projects also spread decay by displacing thousands of very poor households from clearance areas. Until the mid-1960s, such spreading decay involved great overcrowding in the neighborhoods newly "invaded" by the poor. There was little abandonment at the center because of continued natural increase, in-migration, and rebuilding through renewal.

Recently, slowing birth rates, falling in-migration, stronger urban renewal relocation requirements, and accelerated housing production have modified this process. Instead of being pushed out of crisis ghetto areas by expanding populations or urban renewal, poor households now move into surrounding areas because of the negative conditions in crisis ghettos plus the availability of alternative housing nearby. This availability in turn depends upon rising vacancy in the metropolitan area as a whole. Thus the spreading of urban decay in inner-city neighborhoods is an almost inescapable result of large-scale new construction of housing anywhere within a metropolitan area, as long as the impact of that new construction is not offset by demolitions or rapid total population growth. We can expect that continuation of the record housing construction levels of 1971 and 1972—as called for by the 1968 Housing and Urban Development Act—will stimulate rapid spreading of inner-city decay unless specific offsetting policies are undertaken.

Exactly the same linkage underlies another key conclusion: no major displacement of low-income households can occur except in a relatively "loose" overall housing market. When housing markets are "tight," it is difficult to find adequate relocation housing for low-income households displaced by public projects. All the "decent" units available on the private market are quickly rented or bought by middle- and upper-income households, who can outbid the poor. New public housing units are rapidly filled from natural increases in the low-income population. In a "tight" housing market, as a result, displacement of the poor to facilitate renewal or other public projects is possible only through deliberate overcrowding. But this violates recent statutes requiring adequate relocation of households displaced by federally financed projects. Therefore, *no significant rehabilitation, renewal, clearance, or other partly publicly financed rebuilding of the nation's crisis ghettos can occur except when "loose" housing market conditions prevail.*[3] Yet those same conditions are likely to generate a spontaneous spreading of urban decay through abandonment of housing in crisis ghettos and "invasion" of surrounding neighborhoods.

How Individual Upgrading Causes Neighborhood Decline

The process referred to above as the "spreading of urban decay" is not considered bad by all the households who participate in it. It involves a paradoxical contrast between quality-of-environment changes in individual households and those in whole neighborhoods. Many poor households move out of the crisis ghetto into nearby neighborhoods because they believe conditions in the latter are much better. In contrast, the households initially predominating in those nearby neighborhoods—whom I will refer to as the "original" residents—regard the arrival of others from the crisis ghetto as a sign of beginning neighborhood decline. If these newcomers have significantly lower incomes than the original residents, their arrival may cause a drop in the average level of property maintenance, which may lead many original residents to move to other neighborhoods higher up the economic ladder, as described in chapter 1. If more and more households arrive from the crisis ghetto, the entire neighborhood may experience massive transition to dominance by the newcomer group. This produces the following changes in environmental quality, as seen from different viewpoints:

1. Most households moving into the transition neighborhood from the crisis ghetto regard themselves as better off, since conditions are better than where they came from.

2. Most of the original residents of the transition area also regard themselves as better off, since they have moved to somewhat "better quality" neighborhoods elsewhere. However, some may prefer the original environment in the neighborhood they moved from.

3. The quality of environment in the transition neighborhood itself is considered to have deteriorated in the eyes of the original residents (though most have moved away), the initial newcomers (since when they arrived, the area was still mainly occupied by the original, more affluent residents), and the larger urban community (since the average household income level and quality of maintenance in the area have declined).

4. The government of the central city in which these neighborhoods are located (assuming both are in the central city) and all local taxpayers are worse off than before. Deteriorated property conditions have spread to a higher fraction of the central city's neighborhoods, thereby weakening its tax base. Costs of providing fire protection, police protection, and certain other services have probably risen as a result.

5. A significant number of original residents who have been unable to move out regard themselves as much worse off than when this transition process began. This group includes many

of the elderly who cannot afford to sell their homes and purchase housing elsewhere.

6. Many of the households still remaining in the crisis ghetto also regard themselves as much worse off than before. More housing abandonment has occurred around them and many mainstream poor have moved out.

Thus most individual households directly involved in such transition believe they have improved their environments, though households "trapped" in both areas believe the opposite. At the same time, most people in the community believe the quality of neighborhood environment has deteriorated in *both* the crisis ghetto and the nearby transition area. Finally, the city's fiscal position has probably been worsened. I believe it is reasonable to regard this complex outcome as the "spreading of urban decay." On the other hand, under some conditions, it would be desirable to encourage such neighborhood transition as the most feasible means of making better housing available to low-income households.

PROVIDING VIABLE NEIGHBORHOODS FOR CRISIS GHETTO RESIDENTS

Improving the conditions of life now experienced by most crisis ghetto residents is an extremely complex process that no one fully understands how to accomplish. However, one of the necessary ingredients is to create a viable neighborhood environment for these households. As pointed out in chapter 9, providing crisis ghetto residents with viable neighborhoods means shifting them from living in mainly poor areas to living in mainly middle-class areas. Theoretically, there are only three ways this can be done:

1. *Recapturing the middle class.* Middle- and upper-income households can be brought back into crisis ghettos in sufficient numbers so they become the dominant group there.

2. *Dispersal.* Present poor residents of crisis ghettos can be moved into other now predominantly middle-class areas in such a way that those areas will not lose middle-class dominance.

3. *Enrichment without movement.* Present poor residents of crisis ghettos can be economically upgraded out of poverty without leaving their existing neighborhoods. If enough presently poor residents rise to middle-income status, their neighborhoods would presumably become middle-income dominated, even if some households there were still poor.

Each of these key strategies is discussed below in detail so as to determine its relationship to opening up the suburbs.

Recapturing the Middle Class

Most big-city mayors faced with expanding urban decay advocate recapturing the middle class as the best remedy. But widespread experience shows that middle- and upper-income households—white, black, or other—will not move into areas now considered crisis ghettos until after a drastic alteration of the whole environment there. A new milieu must be produced that is simultaneously (1) physically renewed, (2) socially and economically dominated by middle-income households, and (3) provided with good quality public services. This means there cannot be any gradual transition of crisis ghettos from present dominance by low-income households to future dominance by middle-income ones through steady replacement of the former by the latter. Without tangible evidence of large-scale, all-at-once renewal, almost all middle-income households will exercise their ability to choose other places to live.

True, a few once-decayed urban neighborhoods have been "spontaneously" renewed through gradual reoccupation by upper-income households. Examples are Georgetown in Washington, D.C., Old Town in Chicago, and Rittenhouse Square in Philadelphia. But these experiences cannot be duplicated in most American crisis ghettos. These showcase areas are very small, are close to some major employment, educational, or entertainment concentration that sustained resale demand for housing there, were reoccupied primarily by wealthy households who could afford high rehabilitation costs and private schools, and were generally not surrounded by other crisis ghettos. Moreover, initial private rehabilitation in these areas has been strongly supported by later public renewal efforts.

If recapturing the middle class requires completely renovating big chunks of existing crisis ghetto areas, most of the many poor households now living in those chunks will have to move somewhere else. Either they will be displaced as part of the renovation, or they will already have abandoned the area spontaneously before renovation. Where will these poor households go? They must either move into adjacent neighborhoods or take advantage of subsidized housing deliberately dispersed throughout the metropolitan area. Their movement into adjacent neighborhoods in large numbers is likely to initiate urban decay there, as described earlier. Thus, recapturing the middle class cannot be used to renovate crisis ghettos unless it is preceded by either a spreading of urban decay to adjacent areas or a deliberate dispersal policy.

Furthermore, rebuilding crisis ghettos by recapturing the middle class creates a double-barreled political threat to elected officials. On the one hand, it requires displacing the poor—who clearly have the most pressing housing needs—and creating new publicly subsidized housing for the more affluent—even though they already enjoy adequate housing. That is a bitter pill for low-income voters to swallow. In fact, their refusal to accept it has blocked major urban renewal projects in crisis ghettos for several years. They might not oppose such renovation if they were offered decent subsidized housing somewhere else in which to relocate. Even if the specific households displaced by renovation did not move directly into this relocation housing, such an expansion of the total low-income housing supply might be a politically acceptable response to their needs.

But where would these additional units for the poor be located? Nearly every neighborhood outside the crisis ghetto vehemently objects to relocating the poor within its boundaries, because residents fear this supposed first step toward transforming their area into a crisis ghetto. So the only way to persuade the poor to accept the required relocation—dispersal—arouses strong hostility among the non-poor. It is therefore not surprising that improving crisis ghettos by recapturing the middle class has remained a largely rhetorical strategy. Until it is combined with deliberate dispersal of low- and moderate-income housing throughout the metropolitan area, it has little chance of adoption anywhere. Of course, if a city simply waited until its worst crisis ghettos had become almost completely abandoned, major renovation could occur without displacing many people. But even those areas with the greatest abandonment still have thousands of residents. Near-total abandonment would take a long time—if it ever occurred. By then, spreading urban decay would have created new crisis ghettos in many adjoining neighborhoods—which means that waiting for complete abandonment without dispersal before trying to recapture the middle class cannot reduce the *net amount* of urban decay.

Dispersal

Moving poor residents out of crisis ghettos into presently middle-class dominated areas elsewhere is the second method of enabling them to live in viable neighborhoods. Such movement must be carried out so it does not simply shift crisis ghetto conditions to the other areas. This means the number of low- and moderate-income households entering middle-income neighborhoods must be kept between two limits. It must be absolutely large enough to give the incoming households a sense of identity and solidarity, to make their votes important to local politicians, and to be noticeable to local middle- and upper-income residents. But it must also be a small enough percentage so that middle-class behavior patterns remain dominant and middle- and upper-income households there and elsewhere do not conclude that the area will soon become dominated by low- and moderate-income occupancy.

Unless cities adopt explicit legal mechanisms for establishing a desired "balance" between households of different income levels (as discussed in chapter 11), it will be difficult to limit the influx of low- and moderate-income households in neighborhoods right next to crisis ghettos. The strong desire to flee from these ghettos will motivate many poor households to enter adjacent areas. Past experiences when such entry led to complete transition of adjacent areas will motivate many middle-income households living there to depart soon and will inhibit other middle-income households from moving in. The resulting sharp drop in middle-income demand in the area will make housing relatively less expensive than elsewhere for low-income households moving from the nearby crisis ghetto, which will reinforce their natural tendency to move to adjacent neighborhoods because of greater familiarity and convenience. Therefore, simply continuing the long-established practice of having out-migrants from crisis ghettos move into adjacent neighborhoods will probably not result in viable neighborhoods for most of those out-migrants in the long run.

That is why providing present crisis ghetto residents with viable neighborhoods requires a metropolitan-area-wide strategy with at least two key ingredients. One is adopting mechanisms that limit or at least discourage their entry into adjacent neighborhoods so as to prevent those areas from being transformed into crisis ghettos too. But this cannot be accomplished unless the other ingredient is provided first: creation of subsidized housing for such households in many mainly middle-income neighborhoods not adjacent to crisis ghettos. Specific rules for the occupancy of those scattered units must be developed so that a certain percentage of their occupants will have moved directly out of the central city. Otherwise, nearly all directly subsidized suburban housing may be occupied by households who already live in the suburbs or are newly formed there. The effectiveness of this strategy for improving inner-city neighborhoods directly thus depends upon opening up the suburbs.

If dispersal were undertaken at a significant scale, what would happen to crisis ghettos and the people left behind there? It is unlikely that even greatly accelerated dispersal would soon cause existing crisis ghettos to disappear or even to shrink much—though it might halt their growth. Therefore, dispersal alone cannot be considered an effective short-range remedy to the problems of crisis ghettos. Nevertheless, I believe it is a necessary ingredient in any such remedy. Possibly effective overall policies regarding crisis ghettos are briefly discussed in chapters 12 and 14.

Enrichment without Movement

Upgrading crisis ghettos without having many of their present residents move somewhere else is the goal of this third strategy. Unlike the other two, it does not appear to require middle-class households outside crisis ghettos to immediately accept some low- and moderate-income households as neighbors. Crisis ghettos are now dominated by low-income households. Transforming them into viable neighborhoods would require significantly raising the incomes of enough local residents so that a majority became middle-income households. (Just raising their incomes might not alter existing behavior patterns enough to produce viable neighborhoods. However, this point is not relevant to the analysis in this section.) Doing this would require higher income maintenance for those who cannot work, creation of relatively well-paying jobs for those who can work but are now unemployed, and upgrading the jobs of many who are already working. I refer to these policies as *non-capital enrichment* because they involve spending directly on people rather than on creating physical capital like housing, schools, and roads.

Non-capital enrichment big enough to create middle-class dominance in these areas would be extremely expensive. It would cost far more than either Congress or the administration has ever been willing to spend in such areas. (This is also true of the other two strategies described above, however. There is no inexpensive way to significantly improve crisis ghettos.) Furthermore, substantially raising the incomes of crisis ghetto residents would cause large numbers of them—especially the mainstream poor—to immediately move somewhere else in order to escape their present environments. Thus this strategy contains a fundamental inconsistency. Most households with incomes high enough to be considered middle class will not voluntarily remain in a crisis ghetto. Since enrichment thus generates movement, enrichment without movement is a contradiction.

However, since upgraded crisis ghetto residents will stay there if they have nowhere else to go, enrichment without movement could work if there were an acute housing shortage in the metropolitan area as a whole. In most American metropolitan areas there has been no overall housing shortage serious enough to accomplish this result for several years. In fact, the massive housing production of 1971 and 1972 has resulted in a temporary oversupply in many areas. Making this strategy feasible would require drastically cutting national housing production, which would be directly opposed to the national housing goal adopted by Congress in 1968 and calling for continued high production through 1978. In addition, reestablishing shortage conditions would raise the cost of housing for *all* urban households. It hardly seems likely that Congress would permit a reversal of present policies drastic enough to make this strategy work.

Another drawback of non-capital enrichment alone is its reliance upon the responsiveness of private markets to improve physical conditions in crisis ghettos. In theory, once the residents had higher incomes, they could pay more for housing, trash removal, and other services. As they bid up the prices of those things, private markets would supposedly respond by supplying more good quality products. But this requires initially escalating prices of all available good quality housing within crisis ghettos to exorbitantly high levels. It would also take a long time to convince private investors to start building new housing there—so long that most upgraded residents would rather move to other good quality areas than wait.

Non-capital enrichment could be expanded to include large *capital* spending for new housing and other physical improvements for the existing residents, using public subsidies and renewal powers. In theory, such all-out enrichment would provide the residents of crisis ghettos with both higher incomes and the type of physical environment more appropriate to those incomes, so they might remain.

Yet no large-scale physical improvements can be carried out in crisis ghettos without major displacement of existing residents or prior abandonment by them—as pointed out earlier. Hence expanding this strategy to include capital enrichment does not remove its fundamental inconsistency. It is not possible to renovate crisis ghettos through either capital enrichment or non-capital enrichment or both without generating major outward movements of people who now live there. The only conceivable exceptions are if tight housing markets prevail (which is very unlikely in the near future—and would probably make capital enrichment impossible by blocking relocation) or if enrichment were delayed until spontaneous abandonment had almost emptied these areas (in which case the same out-movements would already have occurred).

The Decay Containment Strategy

Faced by the above realities, many public policy-makers may decide not to make any serious effort to help residents of existing crisis ghettos live in viable neighborhoods. They may conclude that doing so would be too expensive or would require actions they consider unacceptable (such as opening up the suburbs). Instead they may shift to what I call the *decay containment* strategy. It involves doing little about improving conditions in crisis ghettos but rather trying to confine those conditions to as small an area as possible. Undoubtedly, few political leaders would ever admit choosing such a strategy. But their real choice should be judged by their actions rather than their words. In my opinion, this strategy has already been chosen implicitly by most American city governments, since it represents their dominant policy toward crisis ghettos. Will it work?

The answer depends mainly upon the overall supply/demand balance in each metropolitan-area housing market. Where the overall housing market is very "tight" because of a relative housing shortage, decay containment might succeed. Residents seeking to leave crisis ghettos would have difficulty finding vacant housing elsewhere, because a strong middle-income demand for housing in adjacent neighborhoods would be sustained by the general shortage. This was the situation in many big cities before 1950, but it no longer prevails anywhere in the United States. Creating such shortages would require drastic cuts in recent levels of housing production, in direct contradiction of official national housing policy, as noted above. Furthermore, the federal government has relied upon the housing industry to help stimulate peacetime prosperity; so cutting back housing production might have serious national economic consequences. Finally, a housing shortage severe enough to contain low-income households within existing crisis ghettos would terrifically aggravate tensions in adjacent areas. Low-income households trying to escape crisis ghetto environments would be vying for scarce housing with the original residents and other middle-income households. If differing ethnic groups were involved, this conflict might lead to interracial violence in large cities. So it certainly does not seem in the public interest to promote or even permit the reemergence of a nationwide housing shortage.

Yet if most metropolitan-area housing markets remain relatively "loose," decay containment cannot succeed. The trickle-down process will provide constantly expanding opportunities for many low-income households to move out of crisis ghettos; abandonment in those areas will steadily increase; and out-movement of households from there mainly into adjacent neighborhoods will spread urban decay through each inner city. Decay containment could be made effective only if accompanied by deliberate dispersal of these out-migrating households throughout the metropolitan area. In the absence of such dispersal, the rate at which urban decay spreads through the inner city will be roughly proportional to the rate at which net new housing production creates an overall market surplus in the metropolitan area (though the growth of decay may lag somewhat behind the net production of new units). This is happening right now in many American metropolitan areas.

This process would be modified by resumption of large-scale in-migration of poor households into the inner city from rural areas or abroad. In that case, there would be little or no inner-city abandonment. The arrival of these in-migrants might even produce an acute inner-city housing shortage. But this type of "bottom-upward" shortage would hasten the spread of urban decay by generating strong pressures for outward expansion of the poor from the center of the crisis ghetto. (In contrast, a "top-downward" shortage caused by lower production of high-cost housing would generate strong pressures from outside crisis ghettos inward, thereby impeding the spread of urban decay.) I doubt that such large-scale in-migration will soon resume. But even if it did, decay containment would not work as long as net new construction of housing everywhere in the metropolitan area outpaced total household growth there.[4]

SOME CONCLUSIONS

The following key conclusions emerge from the above analysis:

1. It is impossible to transform crisis ghettos into viable neighborhoods without large-scale movements of low-income households presently living there into other neighborhoods elsewhere.

2. It is impossible to provide the existing residents of crisis ghettos with viable neighborhoods *anywhere* without large-scale movements by many of them into other neighborhoods elsewhere.

3. There are two basic types of outward movements of present crisis ghetto residents. *Spontaneous movement* into other relatively old neighborhoods adjacent to crisis ghettos tends to make those neighborhoods non-viable too, thereby spreading urban decay. More widespread *dispersal* of out-moving residents into subsidized housing throughout the metropolitan area would require some type of deliberate dispersal policy.

4. Thus, all the potentially most effective ways of both transforming crisis ghettos into viable neighborhoods and providing the present residents of crisis ghettos with viable neighborhoods require dispersal—that is, opening up the suburbs along the lines proposed by this book.

5. Anyone who opposes opening up the suburbs is thereby

implicitly opposing any effective means of improving big-city crisis ghetto conditions. Conversely, anyone who favors improving those conditions is thereby implicitly favoring opening up the suburbs.

6. Any continuation of new housing production large enough to keep housing markets "loose" will promote the spread of inner-city decay—unless it is accompanied by the type of dispersal policies described in this book. This will be true even if no attempts whatever are made to improve crisis ghettos directly. Even if a dispersal policy is adopted, urban decay will probably still spread somewhat, unless entirely new mechanisms are developed to "manage" the process of neighborhood abandonment in crisis ghettos. Such mechanisms are discussed in chapter 12.

12 Principles of a Strategy of
Dispersed Economic Integration

I believe America's suburbs should be opened up through a strategy of *dispersed economic integration*. This means a process of achieving greater intermixture of low- and moderate-income households in many different parts of each metropolitan area almost simultaneously. It involves mainly incremental but accelerated changes in existing processes and institutions. This strategy is only one part of what should eventually become a more comprehensive strategy for urban development in each metropolitan area—one that differs greatly, I hope, from our present implicit trickle-down strategy. However, formulating such an overall urban strategy is fantastically complex conceptually. It is also terribly difficult politically. Therefore, we should not wait for one or more new overall urban development strategies to appear before starting to open up the suburbs. Rather, determining how to open up the suburbs effectively should be a key step in designing such a broader strategy. This chapter presents the basic principles of a strategy of dispersed economic integration.

Unfortunately, nearly everyone responds to the words *dispersed* or *economic integration* with the same erroneous mental image. Each visualizes a compulsory, almost overnight shift of millions of poor people—mostly black—directly out of central-city slums into practically every residential block in suburbia. This hypothetical image repels almost everyone. Central-city blacks see it suddenly dissipating their growing political strength. Suburban whites envision their quiet neighborhoods invaded by gangs of welfare-supported delinquents. Those skeptical of government's ability to manage any large-scale undertaking consider it unworkable. Still others view it as cultural chauvinism that would compel millions of poor people to abandon a life style they cherish.

131

Dispersed economic integration as I conceive of it would exhibit none of these traits. Instead, it would involve a speeding up of movement patterns already underway plus initiation of some new ones on a modest scale.

The key principles describing this strategy are shown on an accompanying chart, divided into five groups. Each group can be viewed as means of attaining one of the following five strategic objectives:

1. Establishing a general economic and political climate favorable to this strategy
2. Motivating the key "actors" in the process by providing them with specific economic incentives to perform their functions in it
3. Achieving dispersed economic integration in ways that will preserve suburban middle-class dominance
4. Concurrently improving the quality of life in inner-city areas
5. Relating this strategy to a more comprehensive overall urban development strategy and the institutional mechanisms required to achieve it

The remaining portions of this chapter discuss these five objectives and their corollary principles in detail.

Establishing a Favorable Climate

Dispersed economic integration can best be achieved in a general economic and political climate conducive to making major changes in the trickle-down process of urban development. The following principles show how to help create such a climate.

High level total housing production. When a general housing shortage exists in relation to the market demand for it, competition from middle- and upper-income households for available decent units outside crisis ghettos prevents much deconcentration of the low-income households massed in those ghettos. In theory, subsidized new suburban units could be made available to low- and moderate-income households even during shortage periods. But in fact, it is then difficult to get political support for such subsidies, especially since builders prefer to concentrate on nonsubsidized units when demand for them is high and financing is available. Hence this strategy would be more practicable if annual production of new housing remained high enough to produce relatively "loose" conditions in most metropolitan-area markets. This in turn requires avoidance of tight monetary conditions, of rapid inflation, and of running the overall economy at close to its aggregate production capacity. However, it does not necessarily require meeting the official national housing goal of adding 26 million units from 1968 through 1978. Nor does it require annually matching the record housing outputs of 1971 and 1972.

Support for large direct housing subsidies. Dispersed economic integration requires housing many low- and moderate-income households in brand-new units, since there are no older units in new-growth areas. Moreover, this strategy involves locating thousands of low- and moderate-income households in both new and existing units they cannot afford without public assistance. It therefore requires relatively high levels of direct housing subsidies—preferably a mixture of both new construction-oriented subsidies (such as the Section 235 and 236 programs) and existing inventory-oriented subsidies (such as a housing allowance).

Advocacy by national leaders. I believe most Americans are now opposed to opening up the suburbs, partly because they do not realize the importance of doing so in order to help solve many of our key urban problems. Strong leadership by persons influential in shaping public opinion could therefore be extremely important in generating the political support needed to make this strategy feasible. The president, congressional leaders, governors, mayors, cabinet officers, and leading businessmen and labor union officials could be especially significant. Up to now, few of these officials have shown any inclination to exercise such leadership.

PROVIDING MOTIVATION THROUGH INCENTIVES

The existing structure of economic incentives related to housing and urban development tends to reinforce the trickle-

Principles of a Strategy of Dispersed Economic Integration

Establishing a Favorable General Climate

1. Total housing production must continue at high enough levels to create "loose" housing market conditions in most metropolitan areas.
2. There must be adequate support for housing subsidies to provide a large number of directly subsidized units for low- and moderate-income households each year, including newly constructed units.
3. The nation's political leaders should recognize the need to alter existing urban development processes and help influence public opinion toward accepting such alterations.

Providing Motivation through Specific Incentives

1. All those moving to the suburbs would do so voluntarily.
2. Specific economic incentives should be provided to encourage low- and moderate-income central-city households to move into suburban neighborhoods.
3. Policies should be adopted to increase the receptivity of suburban areas to low- and moderate-income newcomers.
4. Strong economic incentives and many opportunities should be provided to housing developers, builders, and owners to encourage their creation and operation of housing for low- and moderate-income households in many different parts of each metropolitan area.
5. Dispersed economic integration should be part of a larger, comprehensive urban development strategy that offers major long-range benefits to suburban areas.

Preserving Suburban Middle-Class Dominance

1. Initial emphasis should be upon *economic* rather than *racial* dispersed integration.

2. Varied geographic scales of low- and moderate-income concentration should be tested before any are chosen as most appropriate for widespread use.

3. Massive and rapid movements of people should be avoided.

4. Specific efforts should be made to limit the percentage of low- and moderate-income households in most middle-class neighborhoods.

5. Economic integration should occur in many different parts of each metropolitan area almost simultaneously, rather than in just a few suburbs.

6. Initially, a strategy of obstacle-removal and decentralized decision-making should be followed in deciding where to locate subsidized housing in each metropolitan area.

Concurrently Improving Inner-City Areas

1. Top priority should be placed upon more effective crime prevention in both central cities and suburbs.

2. Income maintenance, job creation, and other "consumer empowerment" programs should have higher priority than additional capital investment in physically improving inner-city areas.

3. New means of comprehensively "managing" entire inner-city neighborhoods should be developed to provide a more effective means of withdrawing economic support from housing units that ought to be demolished.

4. Relatively few small-scale physical capital investment projects should be placed in decaying inner-city areas until incomes there are raised and dispersed economic integration is underway. Eventually, large-scale capital investment through urban renewal should be undertaken there.

Relating the Strategy to Long-Run Institutional Change

1. New institutions able to plan and act effectively at the metropolitan-area level should be developed as soon as possible.

2. More comprehensive urban development strategies should be designed to incorporate dispersed economic integration and establish conditions conducive to its success.

down process. For example, black households now living in segregated central-city areas can buy or rent good quality housing less expensively in nearby neighborhoods undergoing massive transition than in more distant all-white suburban areas. Few white home-buyers or renters are willing to enter racial transition areas, so competition for units there is far less intensive than in primarily white suburbs. This often results in blacks finding nearly identical units priced much lower in racial transition areas than elsewhere. In this way they are economically encouraged to perpetuate racial segregation. Several types of incentives are required to overcome this powerful existing incentive structure, as indicated by the following principles:

The voluntary nature of movement in this strategy. In our free society, any households who move as part of this strategy must do so voluntarily. In addition, those who wish to remain in central cities should be able to do so. Although the term *dispersed* may sound manipulative, in no way does this strategy imply "forced migration" of people who do not want to move. That is why strong incentives for participation are necessary. True, many residents of neighborhoods into which low- and moderate-income households move may oppose such movement, and thus voluntariness applies to those who move, not necessarily to those who already live in destination areas. Moreover, limitations on certain movements will be required under some circumstances. Quantitative targets may have to be used to determine the number or percentage of low- and moderate-income households who can move into specific neighborhoods. When such limitations exist, an individual household's ability to move into a given area would be restricted if its doing so would cause the prescribed target to be exceeded. Finally, many public projects require authorities to acquire and demolish existing housing, thereby involuntarily displacing its residents. However, such displacement should always be *preceded* by adequate relocation assistance.

Providing incentives for out-migration to suburbs. Ironically, one of the most difficult parts of developing effective economic integration will be motivating central-city low- and moderate-income households to move into suburban neighborhoods. Most residents of crisis ghetto areas will not hesitate to move elsewhere if they have a chance. But some will be reluctant to leave central cities. Many black households in particular will want to remain in or near large all-black areas rather than move into largely white neighborhoods. On the other hand, it would be relatively easy to fill all new suburban low- and moderate-income housing with households already living in the suburbs or newly forming there. Yet the basic strategy of deconcentrating poverty from the most deprived central-city areas will not work unless thousands of low- and moderate-income households of every ethnic type voluntarily move from such areas into suburbs. Therefore, accessibility to a certain fraction of suburban subsidized housing (say, 20 to 25 percent) should be reserved for households moving out from central-city poverty areas. Furthermore, special "moving adjustment" grants could be made to such households, and job training aids could be linked to entry into suburban subsidized housing (as in British new towns).

Increasing receptivity to low- and moderate-income newcomers in suburban communities. Although many suburbanites now oppose receiving more low- and moderate-income neighbors, it might be possible to convert this antagonism to cooperation by creating financial incentives benefiting suburbs that accept such residents. Possible incentives are mentioned in chapter 14.

A second approach would be to disarm suburban resistance by reducing local government powers to block the entry of low- and moderate-income households. At the same time, poorer families could be provided with the economic capabilities for entering the suburbs. This is discussed more fully later in this chapter.

Providing incentives for developers, builders, and apartment owners. Low- and moderate-income households are not a promising market for any new housing or for most existing housing unless their incomes are supplemented by subsidies. Such subsidies must be provided in forms that motivate builders, developers, and owners of existing apartment units to furnish adequate housing to these households at locations dispersed throughout each metropolitan area. These private entrepreneurs must be able to anticipate high enough profits from their roles in this strategy to compensate them for bearing the many burdens of overcoming local resistance to subsidized housing.

Making dispersed economic integration part of a more comprehensive urban development strategy. A basic principle of conflict settlement is that any party is more likely to accept a short-run disadvantage if it is tied into a longer-range agreement that provides big future advantages.[1] Most suburbanites undoubtedly regard dispersed economic integration as a disadvantage. However, their willingness to accept it might be greatly increased if it were considered part of a longer-range urban development strategy likely to provide them with other outcomes they value highly. Such outcomes could include reduced environmental pollution, lower urban crime rates, more control of suburban sprawl and future residential development, and less likelihood of future massive transition of neighborhoods from all middle-income to all low-income occupancy or from all-white to all-black occupancy. I believe all these outcomes would be made more likely by creation of the planning and decision-making institutions required to achieve dispersed economic integration. Furthermore, if such integration helped to improve inner-city conditions, it might enable suburban politicians to gain more central-city political support for stronger controls over suburban development and environmental pollution. The possibility of receiving such "trade offs" for accepting some suburban economic integration might at least reduce present hostility toward that objective.

Preserving Suburban Middle-Class Dominance

The particular methods used to achieve dispersed economic integration should be designed to preserve existing middle-class dominance in most suburban neighborhoods. The following six principles set forth key ways to achieve this goal:

Initially emphasizing economic rather than racial integration. The integration strategy advocated by the National Advisory Commission on Civil Disorders (the "Kerner Commission") emphasized racial rather than economic integration. Although I helped design that strategy, I now believe the emphasis of public policy should shift to *economic integration* of the suburbs. Public policy ought to focus upon making housing and social services available for *all* low- and moderate-income households in suburban areas, especially where new growth is occurring. At the same time, laws prohibiting racial discrimination in *all* suburban housing should be vigorously enforced, and new institutions and financial aids should be created to help blacks move into suburban housing of all prices. Thus, the shift of emphasis mentioned above does not mean abandoning the goal of greater racial integration outside central cities or specific tactics to achieve that goal. But resistance to new low- and moderate-income neighbors by suburban whites is likely to be greater if they believe those neighbors will be mainly black rather than mainly (though not solely) white. Furthermore, active support for racial integration has declined among black leaders recently, even though polls show most black citizens still desire it. For these reasons, I believe it best to emphasize economic integration at the outset. If not enough racial integration occurs to help counter the tendency toward two separate and unequal societies, then this policy should be changed.

Testing scales of low- and moderate-income concentration. Since we do not know the most appropriate sizes for clusters of low- and moderate-income households in mainly middle-class areas, public policy ought to encourage a variety of cluster sizes before concentrating upon creation of just a few types. Such experimentation should occur within definite limits derived from experience of what scales do *not* work and what conditions constitute a "suitable living environment" for both low- and moderate-income households and their more affluent neighbors. From these limits I have developed the following criteria:

1. In most cases, low- and moderate-income households living in mainly middle-class neighborhoods should be clustered in groups. These groups should be large enough to allow such households to feel some sense of identity with others like

themselves, to provide an immediate neighborhood that is economically homogeneous, and to enable society to provide these households with certain public services more efficiently than complete scatteration would allow. How big must a cluster be to achieve these goals? It could be quite small and still achieve the first two goals—say, five to ten households. But this is probably far too small for economies of scale in providing most special public services for low- and moderate-income households.

2. No newly established cluster of low- and moderate-income households (or set of smaller clusters) should contribute more than 25 percent of the children attending any of the public schools serving it. Nor should any cluster antedating the strategy be expanded so it begins to provide more than 25 percent of local school enrollment.

3. In many suburbs, it will be desirable to keep these clusters small to allow continual daily interaction among households with very different economic levels. This would also prevent established residents from feeling "overwhelmed" by incoming low- and moderate-income households.

4. At the start, a significant number of low- and moderate-income households should be scattered *individually* in middle-income neighborhoods. This would help to determine under what conditions it is unnecessary to group them in a cluster.

5. In some cases, it may prove impossible to provide much additional housing for low- and moderate-income households within reasonable commuting range of suburban job centers without adding to large existing clusters of such households. This might create several undesirably large suburban concentrations of poverty. Nevertheless, *as a last resort,* some such additions would be better than no increase in economic integration.

Avoiding massive movements. Marginally speeding up and modifying existing population movements is initially preferable to massive shifts of population. For one thing, we need far more empirical knowledge of the effects of different sized groupings of low- and moderate-income households in mainly middle-class neighborhoods. Also, we do not know how best to provide such clusters with appropriate social services, or how the effectiveness of these services will be influenced by cluster size and locational patterns. Furthermore, suburbanites are likely to resist economic integration less vehemently if it involves gradual acceleration of present movement patterns.

Advocates of black nationalism and greater black political power will also regard economic integration as less threatening if it does not reduce the number of black central-city residents in its early phases. Such reduction can be avoided if the number of blacks who move out of a central city each year is less than the annual increase that would occur in its black population if there were no dispersed economic integration. Actually, only a small fraction of suburban housing initially made available to low- and moderate-income households would be occupied by blacks. In fact, it is quite possible that a strategy of dispersed economic integration might accelerate the withdrawal of whites from central cities. This outcome would be contrary to a key potential benefit of opening up the suburbs—counteracting tendencies toward two separate but unequal societies. Nevertheless, it must be considered a distinct possibility unless the incentives described above are deliberately provided so as to encourage black out-migration from central cities.

Using quantified mixture targets and other mixture control devices. A crucial part of this strategy must be preventing middle- and upper-income households from perceiving the arrival of a few low- and moderate-income households as the start of an "invasion" that will completely alter their neighborhoods. Hence the strategy must contain devices that will limit the percentage of low- and moderate-income households entering many suburban areas (though not all of them), as discussed in chapter 11.

Blanketing the entire metropolitan area. Low- and moderate-income households should be introduced into nearly all parts of each metropolitan area within a relatively short period of time. Quick attainment of a broad geographic spread is more important than reaching any specific quantitative targets rapidly. It will convince middle- and upper-income households that they cannot escape less affluent neighbors by moving somewhere else in the metropolitan area. They will then be more likely to remain where they are and to begin interacting constructively with their new neighbors.

It is particularly crucial for low- and moderate-income households to move into the newest peripheral suburban growth areas very soon, for this will block the basic middle-class escape pattern of constantly moving farther away from the central city. Therefore it is vital not to confine dispersal to outlying portions of the central city while ignoring the suburbs.

Starting with a decentralized decision-making strategy, while trying to develop effective metropolitan-wide planning and action powers. Throughout each metropolitan area, the urban development process functions as an economic, social, and geographic unity. Yet the political powers needed to respond to and to mold urban development are divided among myriad governmental bodies. Usually none represents the area as a whole. Thus there is no power anywhere within each metropolitan area to plan and execute actions commensurate with the scope of the problems generated by urban development.

Under these conditions, no strategy can effectively shape future urban growth in accordance with a single, cohesive, rational plan. Unified planning and action covering the entire metropolitan area has sometimes been achieved regarding certain specialized functions, like combating air pollution or treating sewage. But it has rarely been achieved concerning housing, land use planning, or provision of residentially related government services.

This failure is no accident. It directly benefits many who would be injured by solutions to certain problems generated by urban development. The most obvious beneficiaries are officials and residents of middle- and upper-income suburbs. If the need for area-wide planning and action were effectively met, they would have to bear more of the costs of metropolitan living. In addition, they might have to share certain benefits that they alone now enjoy, by allowing less affluent citizens to become their neighbors. Most of these people now perceive this change mainly as a net loss, so they strongly oppose any moves to create unified planning and action capabilities for urban development. It is probably unfair to attribute this posture solely to their selfish desire to maintain favored positions. They have a right to influence the quality of their neighborhood environments. Yet is is not clear to them how they could do so if presently divided powers over those environments were shifted to some area-wide body.

Furthermore, most central-city political leaders are equally adamant against yielding any sovereignty to a new higher authority. They realize their communities now pay excessive shares of the costs of metropolitan living. Yet they do not want to sacrifice any influence over their own territories. Black politicians are especially opposed to any shift to metropolitan-wide governance that would rob them of their long-awaited chance to exercise power over central-city governments. In order to avoid such a power shift and still improve their present unfair position, many central-city leaders advocate federal revenue sharing, with cities as direct recipients. This would provide access to suburban-generated tax revenues without compelling them to yield power over their present territories.

Thus, very little support exists *within* metropolitan areas for area-wide planning and action. Most such support has come from "outsiders"—especially federal administrators. Given these circumstances, how can any area-wide strategy for economic integration succeed?

Two approaches are possible. One is to try to establish area-wide institutions in spite of present obstacles. The other is to adopt a decentralized strategy that might create a great deal of low- and moderate-income housing in suburbia, although not in accordance with one cohesive plan. These approaches are not mutually exclusive. Federal officials could promote the decentralized strategy now while trying to generate the institutions needed to carry out the centralized strategy in the long run. I have already described what a centrally planned area-wide strategy might be like. What would a decentralized area-wide strategy be?

The basic idea is to remove obstacles to the entry of low- and moderate-income households into suburban communities, to create economic pressures encouraging their entry, and then to let individual builders and households determine where it will occur. Like present urban development in general, this process would not follow any single area-wide plan. Rather, its results would emerge from thousands of individual decisions made under rules and conditions designed to achieve the desired outcome. Specifically, this strategy would contain the following ingredients (some of which are repeated elsewhere in this chapter):

1. Removing local obstacles to the entry of such households through court suits, tying federal funding for other programs to such removal, or tying federal funding for state programs to passage of statewide laws that removed such obstacles (such as statewide building codes or zoning maps)
2. Developing programs that provide central-city low- and moderate-income households with incentives and resources to enter suburban housing markets
3. Providing strong incentives for home-builders to construct or renovate housing units for low- and moderate-income households throughout suburban areas (many programs offering such incentives already exist)
4. Creating financial incentives to make suburban communities more receptive to low- and moderate-income households
5. Providing large-scale funding for all the above programs

This decentralized strategy of dispersed economic integration both resembles and takes advantage of free markets. It makes the urban development process more like a free market by removing local obstacles to the entry of low- and moderate-income households. It helps such households more closely resemble middle- and upper-income consumers by providing them (and builders serving them) with various subsidies.

In theory, this approach may seem inferior to a centralized

dispersal strategy. The spatial pattern it would produce is accidental and haphazard rather than the result of a single carefully balanced plan. But an area-wide housing planning and action agency would add another layer of bureaucracy to the decision-making process. As a political body, it would be subject to all the wrangling and delays various pressure groups can cause. Even more important, it might become politically dominated by suburban groups opposed to economic integration. Hence the centralized approach might actually produce far less dispersed economic integration than the decentralized approach—particularly in the near future. Therefore, I believe present emphasis should be upon this decentralized approach. However, it would also be wise to try the centralized approach on an experimental basis in a few metropolitan areas to test its effectiveness.

Concurrently Improving Inner-City Areas

A basic theme of this book is that, since suburban exclusiveness has helped to generate undesirable conditions in many inner-city neighborhoods, opening up the suburbs is necessary to improve those neighborhoods. It is therefore appropriate that part of the strategy of dispersed economic integration address means of improving inner-city areas.

Putting top priority on better crime prevention. The single highest priority objective for any urban development strategy should be drastically improving present methods of preventing crimes. The worst aspect of life in crisis ghettos is the insecurity caused by frequent crime and vandalism. In addition, fear of crime and violence is a central cause of the flight of middle- and upper-income households from central cities. I believe it also underlies the racial hostility that many whites feel toward blacks. A Gallup poll in 1972 showed that 41 percent of all Americans were afraid to walk alone at night in their own neighborhoods—49 percent in cities of 50,000 or more. If that fear could be drastically reduced, far more households with economic resources would be willing to remain in central cities and to live in racially integrated neighborhoods. Until then, low-income portions of central cities permeated by insecurity cannot attract the economic and human resources to become viable neighborhoods. In fact, no plans to revitalize stagnant or declining central-city economies can possibly work without great reductions in the fear and insecurity caused by high crime rates. Finally, suburban residents who have fled from rising insecurity in central cities do not want it to follow them. They will surely oppose any economic integration strategy unless it provides persuasive evidence that it will not cause greater crime and vandalism in their neighborhoods.

Unfortunately, I do not know any tactics sure to accomplish this goal. Real success in combating crime would require profound changes in both the system of criminal justice and the nature of life in crisis ghettos. We do not seem to be making much—if any—progress in either respect. But this goal has not received high social priority in our national life, in spite of the large amount of rhetoric about it. Until it does, no strategy will make much headway in coping with the problems discussed in this book.[2]

Giving higher inner-city priority to income improvement and "consumer empowerment" than to physical capital improvements. Some observers criticize any economic integration strategy for spending public resources in relatively affluent suburbs rather than where the most acute deprivation exists. They believe the best way to reduce such deprivation is to spend money improving crisis ghettos directly, and to do so, they recommend massive spending for better housing, health care, job opportunities, income maintenance, schools, police protection, and other services in these areas.

I do not believe this seemingly "direct" approach can work in the long run, because it fails to reduce the concentration of poverty, as discussed in chapters 9 and 11. True, if income maintenance programs were huge enough to eliminate poverty in crisis ghettos, the quality of life there would certainly improve. But *relative* deprivation would not be ended. Also, it might take a long time to alter the existing behavior patterns of low-income multiproblem households.

Under these conditions, is it true that a strategy of dispersed economic integration wrongly diverts massive public resources from crisis ghettos? I think not. For one thing, Congress has recently cut back funding on urban renewal, Model Cities, school aid for the poor, and other programs that primarily aid such areas. Hence the "diversion" issue is largely rhetorical. The concentration of future population and economic growth in suburbs virtually guarantees that most spending on urban development will occur there rather than in central cities. Dispersed economic integration simply tries to ensure that such growth involves a balanced population, not just affluent households.

Even if massive spending in crisis ghettos were politically feasible, no one knows whether it would cure their basic ills. It would certainly not end the dependency of those residents who cannot work. Nor would it be likely to attract into these areas households or businesses with adequate private economic resources. It would assist non-multiproblem poor households— undoubtedly the vast majority—but it might not greatly reduce negative spillover effects from multiproblem households. We simply do not know how to solve many of this group's problems. For these reasons, some people oppose "wasting" *any* resources trying to improve crisis ghettos.

My own view is that three types of activities should be carried out in crisis ghettos without waiting for metropolitan-wide solutions. One is providing a minimum-quality standard of living for the poor everywhere—including such areas. This should be done through nationwide income maintenance and job creation programs, plus certain public service programs such as health care, education, and various forms of counseling. These programs should focus upon upgrading individuals directly, not upon creating physical capital or aiding government agencies. I believe such nationwide "consumer empowerment" programs should have maximum social priority—even higher than opening up the suburbs. They should receive large-scale nationwide funding, mainly from the federal government. The other types of activity we should carry out in inner cities are discussed below.

Developing new forms of "neighborhood management." Recent increases in housing abandonment in crisis ghettos have revealed a major deficiency in the nation's basic strategy of ending physically inadequate housing by flooding the market with new units. This strategy implicitly seeks to depress the economic value of the worst substandard urban housing units by providing modern competition for them, in the hope that those units will fall in value so sharply that they will ultimately be demolished. But experience shows that this strategy does not cope effectively with the negative spillover effects that vacant units awaiting demolition have upon surrounding units that are still physically sound. Units justifiably abandoned because of their poor condition attract addicts, vandals, delinquents, and others whose presence causes households occupying nearby sound units to move out of the area as soon as they can. Once the decent units they were occupying become vacant for even a brief period, they are instantly wrecked by vandals. Areas where such "contagion effects" occur are marked by fragmentalized property ownership plus absence of either adequate security or adequate financing. As a result, there is no present way to carry out an "orderly withdrawal" from the part of the housing inventory that ought to be abandoned without generating abandonment of essentially sound housing nearby.

We need some new form of overall neighborhood management by a single responsible agency, either public or private or a combination of both. Such an agency should be able to protect vacant property from destruction, order rapid demolition of that which ought to be destroyed, repair and maintain that which ought to be preserved regardless of who owns it, arrange necessary financing for these functions, and treat each neighborhood as though it were a single entity rather than a jumble of unrelated properties. At present, no one knows how to perform these functions effectively. Therefore, I believe multiple experiments should be conducted as soon as possible to test different means of doing so, as discussed in chapter 14.

Initial small-scale capital investment in inner-city areas, followed by large-scale urban renewal. At least some specific capital investments should be carried out to produce short-run physical improvements in crisis ghettos. Examples are new housing, housing rehabilitation, better recreation facilities, street lighting, sewer and water systems, and new public buildings. These projects should *not* be undertaken at a very large overall scale. Yet when such projects are proposed by persons or groups with a proven record of success, they should be given enough resources to improve these areas.

In the long run, I doubt that most such projects will be able to withstand the corrosive impacts of continued poverty concentration. Nevertheless, crisis ghettos should not be completely abandoned while we await metropolitan-wide solutions. These areas contain millions of America's most deprived and downtrodden citizens. They deserve attention and resources as a demonstration of their importance, even if the long-range results are not impressive. Moreover, they should have a key voice in determining how such resources are used.

This policy could be condemned as mere tokenism—offering placebos to a truly sick patient. Admittedly, the best medicine for this patient is one that attacks poverty directly. That is why I believe consumer empowerment programs should have higher priority than physical renewal. Furthermore, our limited social capital should be invested in ways that will prove most effective in the long run. Therefore, I recommend focusing subsidized housing for the poor and near-poor in the suburbs where it will help deconcentrate the poor and could eventually create a viable population balance in areas where poor households are now massed together. Placebos should not be scorned, however—they are far better than no medicine at all. There is definite value in indicating to the residents of crisis ghettos that society is willing to invest resources in physically improving their neighborhoods.

Eventually, if poverty becomes sufficiently deconcentrated, crisis ghettos can be redeveloped with large-scale projects that create entirely new neighborhood environments. Enough non-poor residents and other resources could then be attracted to produce an economically integrated environment with middle-class dominance—as required for true viability. But that day will not arrive for most crisis ghettos until poverty there has been greatly deconcentrated by policies like those recommended in this book.

PLANNING A MORE COMPREHENSIVE URBAN DEVELOPMENT STRATEGY

Earlier parts of this chapter discussed the need to relate dispersed economic integration to an even broader overall urban development strategy. It is not within the scope of this book to explore such a comprehensive urban development strategy very fully. Only its main aspects necessary to dispersed economic integration are dealt with in the following principles.

Creating effective metropolitan area-wide planning and action institutions. For reasons stated earlier, I favor a decentralized approach to choosing suburban locations for subsidized low- and moderate-income housing in the near future. However, in the long run, I doubt that much progress can be made toward solving our most serious urban problems without effective area-wide planning and action capabilities. These problems include air pollution, water pollution, inadequate public transportation, low-quality education, high minority-group unemployment, deteriorated housing, high crime rates and vandalism in crisis ghettos, and other negative conditions resulting from concentrated poverty. Courts are already pressing for area-wide approaches to some of these problems. True, the mere creation of area-wide powers will not solve such difficult problems. But unless such powers exist, no other policies or programs can probably solve them either—including revenue sharing. Therefore, although we must now use decentralized strategies as best we can, we should continue strong efforts to create effective area-wide institutions as soon as possible.

Designing more comprehensive urban development strategies to include dispersed economic integration. Comprehensive urban development strategies could certainly be designed without including dispersed economic integration. In fact, America's presently dominant urban development strategy—the trickle-down process—completely excludes dispersed economic integration. Hence an important means of promoting it is by seeking to have its major elements incorporated into any larger urban development strategy in the United States. The first step is describing the chief ingredients of dispersed economic integration and making the potential architects of more comprehensive strategies aware of those ingredients. That is, I hope, one of the main functions of this book.

13 Quantifying the Strategy

If a strategy of dispersed economic integration were adopted, how many low- and moderate-income households would move from central cities to suburbs each year? How many suburban housing units would need to be built for, or occupied by, such households? How many of these housing units would require direct subsidies? The strategy proposed by this book cannot be evaluated without specific answers to these questions. Whether it is sensible and feasible or totally impractical depends upon whether the population movements and housing subsidies it requires could actually be achieved. No reasonable judgments can be made about that without some quantification of those variables.

Consequently, I have prepared rough estimates concerning future changes in the low-income population in central cities and suburbs, future outflows of low-income households required to attain certain target outcomes by 1980, and numbers of housing units of various types that would have to be subsidized to achieve those targets. These estimates should be regarded only as illustrating the order of magnitude of the key variables concerned. They are certainly not reliable bases for detailed public policies. Yet I believe they are accurate enough for an overall evaluation of whether the strategy in this book is basically feasible. I have focused solely upon low-income households, both because more data are available concerning them than concerning moderate-income households and because central-city poverty problems are more closely associated with low-income households.

Background Data and Assumptions

The quantification in this chapter has been based upon the following basic data and assumptions:

1. In America's suburbs in 1970, there were 22.685 million occupied housing units containing 76.3 million

152

persons, or 3.36 per unit. About 5.4 million persons, or 7.1 percent, had incomes below the officially defined poverty levels.

2. Suburbs will capture 75 percent of the nation's total population growth from 1970 to 1980. Their population will increase by 18.450 million.

3. The general dynamism of the American economy will reduce the number of persons in the nation officially considered "poor" at an average rate of 2.65 percent per year from 1970 to 1980. This is a lower rate than the annual average of 3.6 percent from 1960 to 1970.

4. Suburban population growth from 1970 to 1980 plus replacement of suburban housing demolished or otherwise removed from the inventory would require construction of 7.481 million new suburban housing units in this decade.

Defining Strategic Goals

The quantitative implications of opening up the suburbs depend upon what choice is made concerning the desired target percentage of poor persons in total suburban population. The higher the target percentage, the more radical the quantitative implications in relation to recent trends. For purposes of illustration only, I have used a target date of 1980. Four illustrative sets of goals and target percentages for that date are discussed below.

1. *Keeping the absolute number of suburban poor the same in 1980 as in 1970.* Because of the rise in total suburban population, this would result in a decline in the *proportion* of low-income persons from 7.1 percent in 1970 to 5.7 percent in 1980. The latter would be the *minimum* target percentage.

2. *Keeping the percentage of suburban poor the same in 1980 as in 1970 (7.1 percent).* This would require raising their *number* from 5.4 million in 1970 to 6.7 million in 1980.

3. *Equalizing the percentage of poor in both central cities and suburbs by 1980.* This would require reducing the central-city percentage from 12.9 to 7.5 percent, and raising the suburban percentage from 7.1 to 7.5 percent. The latter would be the

target percentage. The suburbs would then contain more poor people than central cities.

4. *Reducing the number of central-city poor by one-half from 1970 to 1980.* This goal seeks significant deconcentration of poverty in central cities within the next decade. The *percentage* of poor in central cities would drop from 12.9 percent in 1970 to 6.2 percent in 1980. This would require a suburban poverty target percentage of 8.4 percent by 1980—the *maximum* target. The suburbs would then contain both a higher percentage and a larger number of low-income persons than central cities.

REQUIRED MIGRATION FLOWS

Attainment of the maximum 8.4 percent suburban poverty target would require an estimated net out-migration of 2.7 million low-income persons from central cities to suburbs during the 1970s. They would constitute 36 percent of the *total* out-migration from central cities to suburbs. In comparison, I estimate that about 500,000 poor persons (net) migrated from central cities to suburbs in the 1960s—or 10 percent of all such migration. Attaining this relatively high suburban poverty target would thus require tremendous increases in the number and percentage of poor persons in total out-migration from central cities. In contrast, achieving the minimum 5.7 percent target would require a net out-migration of only 133,000 low-income persons from central cities to suburbs during the 1970s. This is many fewer than I believe migrated in the 1960s. However, both other targets would require much larger low-income out-migration than occurred in the 1960s.

REQUIRED ALLOCATIONS OF HOUSING

What effect would choice of each target have upon the allocation of suburban housing to low-income households during the 1970s? I will examine in detail how the highest target might be achieved and summarize results for the others.

There will be an estimated 28.276 million occupied suburban housing units in 1980. Achievement of the 8.4 percent target would mean that 2.375 million units would be occupied by low-income households—a net addition of 787,000 units over those so occupied in 1970. Moreover, some of the suburban units occupied by low-income households as of 1970 would be removed from the inventory by 1980. I estimate that a total of 1.259 million additional suburban housing units would have to be made available to low-income households through subsidies to reach this target by 1980.

How many of these subsidized suburban units should receive the large per unit aid required to make *newly built* housing available to the poor? The answer depends upon the degree of economic integration society wishes to achieve in new-growth suburban areas. Let us assume first that *none* of the additional suburban housing made available to low-income households in the 1970s consists of newly built units. Then no poor households will reside in new-growth areas; all the suburban poor will live in older existing suburban areas.

By 1980, total suburban population will have risen 18.450 million over its 1970 level. I arbitrarily assume that 25 percent of this increase will occur through rising density in existing suburban areas and 75 percent through development of new-growth areas. Hence new-growth areas will contain 13.838 million people by 1980—one-seventh of the *entire* suburban population. But they will have zero percent occupancy by low-income households under the above assumption. In order for suburbia as a whole to reach the 8.4 percent target for low-income occupancy, about 9.9 percent of the population of suburban areas built before 1970 would have to consist of poor people. This would result in a striking economic imbalance between the new-growth one-seventh of suburbia and the remaining six-sevenths—much greater than the present imbalance between suburbs and central cities.

To avoid such an imbalance, some newly built suburban housing will have to be made directly available to low-income households. A reasonable target would be provision of enough new suburban units to poor households so that new-growth areas *and* older existing areas in suburbia would *all* average the target low-income occupancy level of 8.4 percent. This would require 352,000 newly built units (27 percent of the low-income suburban total) located in new-growth suburbs and

907,000 units (73 percent) located in existing suburban areas. Most of the latter would be older existing units, but some should be new to use vacant land in built-up areas and to provide a greater variety of housing types. I will arbitrarily assume 25 percent will be new. Added to those in new-growth suburbs, this makes a total of 578,000 *new* housing units for low-income occupancy in *all* suburban areas from 1970 to 1980, or an average of 57,875 per year. All these units would require high per unit subsidies. The 680,250 additional *existing* suburban units to be occupied by low-income households would require smaller—but still significant—per unit subsidies.

How sensible do these targets appear in relation to current levels of housing production and direct subsidy? The 8.4 percent target calls for directly subsidizing an additional 57,875 new and 68,025 existing housing units per year in suburban areas for low-income households, or a total of 125,900. In 1971, 433,480 new units received direct federal subsidies—an all-time record. Probably a maximum of one-fourth, or 108,000 units, were located in suburbs. Moreover, most were for moderate-income households, not low-income ones. Attainment of this target would therefore require (1) shifting much more emphasis to low-income households, (2) maintaining a high level of annual increases in total units subsidized, (3) shifting more of those units from central cities to suburbs, and (4) *reducing* the percentage of new units in the total number directly subsidized—perhaps through a housing allowance. On the other hand, these targets are not unreasonably large in relation to what actually happened in 1971. In fact, reaching this maximum target would require creating only about 13 percent more directly subsidized units each year than may have been built in the suburbs during 1971.

I have presented this analysis in detail to illustrate the methodology involved and to prove the crucial conclusions stated below. There is no need to repeat the process for the other three targets. The analysis of all four is summarized in table 5.

Table 5
Housing Allocations to Attain Various Percentage Targets of Low-Income Persons in Suburban Population by 1980
(All housing unit figures in millions)

		Target Percentages of Low-Income Persons in Total 1980 Suburban Population			
		5.7%	*7.1%*	*7.5%*	*8.4%*
A	Basic goal of target by 1980	Constant number of suburban poor	Constant % of suburban poor	Equal % of city and suburban poor	50% reduction in 1970 number of cen-tral-city poor
B	Total suburban housing units occupied, 1980	28.276	28.276	28.276	28.276
C	Target number of total units for low-income occupancy, 1980	1.612	2.008	2.121	2.375
D	1970 number of low-income occupied units	1.588	1.588	1.588	1.588
E	Additional such units needed by 1980 (C − D)	.024	.420	.533	.787
F	Low-income units to re-place removals	.472	.472	.472	.472
G	Total added low-income units needed (E + F)	.496	.892	1.005	1.259
H	Annual rate of addition, 1970–80	.050	.089	.101	.126

Table 5 (*Continued*)

*Target Percentages of Low-Income Persons
in Total 1980 Suburban Population*

		5.7%	7.1%	7.5%	8.4%
I	Total added units for all income groups in new-growth areas	4.193	4.193	4.193	4.193
J	Target number of units for low-income occupancy in new-growth areas	.239	.298	.314	.352
K	Percentage of total additional low-income need in new-growth areas	48.1%	33.4%	31.2%	28.0%
L	Percentage in existing sub-urban areas	51.9%	66.6%	68.8%	72.0%

THE KEY: ADEQUATE OUT-MIGRATION OF THE POOR

The annual rates of subsidizing additional suburban housing units for low-income households necessary to carry out this strategy are feasible—given recent high levels of total direct housing subsidies. However, the most difficult part of executing this strategy would be generating large enough net outflows of central-city low-income households. Relatively large increases in such out-migration are needed to achieve the strategy's targets. Therefore, if it is to succeed, much attention must be devoted to creating incentives that will encourage low-income households to move out of central cities into the suburbs.

14   Policies and Tactics

The basic strategy described earlier can be achieved if society adopts ten key policies and the tactics to implement it. A *policy* is a broad objective plus a general approach to achieving it. (Many of the policies described in this chapter are similar to specific strategic principles set forth in chapter 12.) *Tactics* are specific actions or programs useful in carrying out a policy. Others might define the required policies and tactics differently. However, I believe my formulation provides an adequate basis for discussion.

In some cases, the tactics linked to a given policy are not consistent with each other. Comprehensive tactics may encompass narrower ones. Some involve radical changes in the status quo; others call for modest changes. Some complement each other; others are alternatives. Hence, *all* tactics listed under each policy should not necessarily be carried out simultaneously.

This "catalog" of policies and tactics has four important limitations:

1. It does not cover all major urban problems but focuses upon those directly related to opening up the suburbs.
2. It contains no relative priorities for either policies or tactics.
3. It merely names possible tactics without describing, costing out, or analyzing each.
4. It does not assess the political feasibility of each policy or tactic. However, chapter 16 contains a general discussion of how political support might be mustered for the strategy.

Escalating Key Decision-Making Powers

Essential to *any* effective urban growth strategy is raising certain presently fragmented decision-making powers to higher levels of government—preferably to the metropolitan-area level. Specific tactics are:

1. Establishing multifunction metropolitan development agencies[1]
2. Establishing single-purpose metropolitan agencies (such as a transportation agency covering both highways and public transportation)
3. Pooling federal transportation and land-use planning funds (including those for several transportation modes)
4. Creating minimum sizes for government bodies exercising zoning powers
5. Consolidating small suburban communities into larger ones
6. Creating metropolitan agencies with stronger review, amendment, and veto powers over lower level decisions (such as the Twin Cities Metropolitan Council)
7. Using federal revenue sharing as an incentive for adoption of changes like those above

Encouraging Larger Scale Urban Development

If urban development occurs in large-sized "chunks" instead of in small subdivisions, economic integration will be easier to achieve in new-growth suburbs and in redeveloped older areas. Developers of larger projects have more economic "elbow room" for low- and moderate-income units that are less profitable than market-oriented units. They can also include several income groups in their projects without causing middle-class residents to lose dominance. Therefore, another basic policy is encouraging urban development at a relatively large geographic scale—larger than at present. When a single developer controls a large area (say, 1,000 acres), he creates one comprehensive plan for all of it. This "internalizes"—and thus takes better account of—spillover effects among different land uses that separate owners would consider beyond their control. Specific tactics are:

1. Designating certain zones for minimum-scale private development
2. Stronger funding of Title VII aid to new communities, and broadening its applicability to certain planned unit developments
3. Creating and funding state urban development corporations
4. Publicly acquiring land and performing predevelopment preparation for subsequent sale or lease to developers
5. More closely controlling private development through sewer and water regulations
6. Creating larger subsidies for big-scale urban renewal projects

CREATING PRESSURES FOR DEVELOPMENT OF LOW- AND MODERATE-INCOME HOUSING

Because such housing is now opposed by most suburbs, a vital policy is creating strong outside pressures on communities throughout each metropolitan area to accept low- and moderate-income housing and strong incentives for market forces and other agencies to supply it. These pressures can remove obstacles to such housing, require it as a prerequisite to other benefits, or create positive incentives for its construction. Specific tactics are:

1. Adopting required "development targets" for low- and moderate-income housing in all new residential developments above some minimum size (such as 25 units)
2. Conducting legal attacks upon exclusionary zoning
3. Removing all special local approval requirements for subsidized housing
4. Regionalizing central-city public housing authority powers to the metropolitan area-wide scale
5. Formulating regional public housing programs
6. Requiring effective low- and moderate-income housing programs as a prerequisite to locating new public or publicly financed facilities in a community

7. Requiring effective low- and moderate-income housing programs for obtaining all types of federal financial aid

8. Continuing high-level funding for builders to take initiatives in creating low- and moderate-income housing

PROVIDING INCENTIVES TO HOUSEHOLDS

A key policy is providing financial and other assistance to low- and moderate-income households as incentives for them to move into suburban neighborhoods. Specific tactics are:

1. Creating a housing allowance
2. Continuing high-level funding of subsidies for new units for low- and moderate-income households (especially since new units are essential in integrating new-growth areas)
3. Providing counseling services to low- and moderate-income households
4. Creating housing information and counseling centers

IMPROVING ACCESSIBILITY OF SUBURBAN JOB OPPORTUNITIES

Lower income households will be more likely to move to the suburbs if they receive prior exposure to suburban job markets. Moreover, their long-run suburban residency will not be feasible without public transportation. Hence a basic policy is improving the accessibility of suburban job opportunities to low- and moderate-income households living in both central cities and suburbs. Specific tactics are:

1. Creating area-wide job information centers in low-income central-city neighborhoods
2. Increasing enforcement effectiveness of equal opportunity programs among suburban employers
3. Subsidizing improved public transportation in suburban areas
4. Experimenting with subsidized car pools and rental arrangements for suburban low- and moderate-income households

Reducing the Adverse Economic Impacts on Suburbs

A central policy is reducing the adverse economic impacts of low- and moderate-income households upon existing suburban residents by changing taxation structures and providing financial aids. Specific tactics are:

1. Shifting all costs of welfare programs to the federal government
2. Equalizing school financing costs
3. Shifting more local school costs to federal or state governments
4. Providing "bonus" financing to local school districts with low- and moderate-income children
5. Providing special community service funding to areas accepting additional low- and moderate-income housing
6. Developing property value insurance for homeowners near low- and moderate-income housing

Developing Population Balancing Mechanisms

A crucial policy is developing means of arriving at and maintaining stable population balances at various geographic scales, as discussed in chapter 10. Specific tactics are:

1. Dividing each metropolitan area into commuting zones for achieving a balance between housing and jobs
2. Using zoning controls to achieve spatial balance of housing types within school districts
3. Adopting state laws requiring a certain percentage of land devoted to low- and moderate-income housing in each community
4. Developing economic-class zoning ordinances
5. Shifting to metropolitan area-wide school attendance planning

Reducing the Size of the Housing Subsidy Gap

A key policy is reducing the size of the housing subsidy gap for low- and moderate-income households by lowering the cost of occupying "decent" housing or the quality level considered "decent." Specific tactics are:

1. Adopting state-wide building and housing codes
2. Using modular or mobile homes for public housing
3. Adopting multi-quality-level housing codes, including lower cost quality levels for lower income housing units
4. Developing a residential maintenance assistance program
5. Encouraging urban renewal authorities to rent rather than sell land
6. Exempting rehabilitation and modernization from local property taxes
7. Removing union requirements for repair and maintenance programs

ATTACKING NEGATIVE CONDITIONS IN AREAS OF POVERTY

What happens in the suburbs cannot be divorced from what happens in central-city poverty areas. Therefore, a fundamental policy should be trying to improve adverse living conditions in urban areas of concentrated poverty. The problems there are so complex and intertwined and so intractable that no short catalog of tactics can describe how to attack them effectively. Some of the tactics set forth above would help improve conditions in these areas. The following are merely illustrative of others that might be tried:

1. Expanding income maintenance
2. Creating employment opportunities
3. Providing counseling for poor households
4. Providing more extensive and effective drug addiction prevention and rehabilitation programs
5. Using civilian police auxiliaries for surveillance in high-crime areas
6. Modernizing and greatly expanding local court systems
7. Using security-conscious physical design and layout principles to inhibit crime in public housing projects[2]

INCREASING AWARENESS AMONG ALL CITIZENS OF THEIR RESPONSIBILITIES

Most suburbanites do not realize how their exclusion of the poor helps create and perpetuate the central-city problems they abhor. On the other hand, many residents of central-city poverty areas are unwilling to confront their own responsibilities for those problems. They cannot expect to enjoy the amenities of middle-class neighborhoods without changing some of their own behavior patterns. Because of the erroneous and incomplete perceptions of both groups, a key policy is increasing awareness among all urban citizens of their particular roles and responsibilities in the urban development process and in solving the problems it generates. This requires enlightened and forceful leadership from persons who understand those roles and responsibilities and can spread that understanding through various media. Specific tactics for this policy will depend mainly upon the strength of our national will to execute the basic strategy in this book. That is discussed in the final two chapters.

15 Some Likely Objections to Opening Up the Suburbs

I have tried to present the arguments for and against opening up the suburbs objectively, even though I clearly favor this strategy. In the same spirit, I here present six likely criticisms of the strategy that differ from the sources of opposition in chapter 7. After each argument, I set forth my own view of its validity.

1. *Opening up the suburbs would spoil the hard-won "sanctuary" of the middle class.* Most suburbanites have sought outlying communities to escape the maladies of big-city living. Opening up the suburbs would help those maladies follow them. It would therefore ruin the quality of life they have worked so hard to develop.

COMMENT. The suburban sanctuary of the middle class has been created at the expense of the urban poor by compelling them to live in areas of concentrated poverty. This forced concentration is one of the main causes of big-city maladies. Hence the remedy adopted by the middle class is really a major cause of the problems it is supposed to cure. The beneficiaries of this remedy therefore have an obligation to counteract the maladies they have helped force upon the urban poor. This book has suggested several ways of doing so without "ruining" the quality of life in predominantly middle-class neighborhoods.

2. *Members of different economic classes do not want to interact with each other and will not do so even if they live in the same neighborhoods.* Residential segregation by economic class has dominated most urban settlements throughout history. One reason is that most poor people feel more comfortable living and interacting with other poor than with wealthier people. Thus economic-class segregation is not just a result of middle-class or upper-class

snobbery. Mixing different economic groups in the same neighborhoods will not change this behavior pattern.

COMMENT. There is undoubtedly some truth in this criticism. However, it assumes that opening up the suburbs means achieving economic integration *only at the personal interaction scale.* On the contrary, the strategy advocated in this book involves three different geographic scales of economic mixture. The scale I believe should be adopted everywhere (that involving access to suburban jobs) does *not* require economic mixture within individual neighborhoods. Moreover, I believe our society should seek to break down historic interaction barriers among economic groups as part of our encouraging greater appreciation of diversity.

3. *The risk that economic integration will fail to achieve any "positive up-lift impact" upon low- and moderate-income households is too great to justify the tremendous costs and effort required to achieve such integration.* We do not even know how to structure interaction between poor and non-poor suburbanites so as to maximize chances that positive contacts will occur.

COMMENT. This criticism also erroneously equates opening up the suburbs with achieving economic integration *only* at the personal interaction scale. That economic integration providing access to jobs and to public schools would produce "positive up-lift impacts" has been repeatedly demonstrated in practice. Moreover, most low- and moderate-income households would greatly benefit from *leaving* crisis ghettos regardless of what "positive up-lift" their new surroundings provided.

4. *The hidden goal of residential economic integration is long-run achievement of a homogeneous society in which all different groups have been thoroughly assimilated. This is a liberal dream inconsistent with the group pluralism on which America has been built.* We neither can nor should counteract the "natural" tendency of most Americans to live in separate clusters, each of which mainly contains people of a certain nationality, or religion, or race, or economic class, or some combination of these. Current sociological research emphasizes how important the separate identities and traditions of these groups are in developing

individually sound personalities among their members. Black nationalism, the most recent example, was preceded by traditions of the Jews, Irish, Italians, and many other ethnic groups. The concept of "integration" implies an ideal of a "fully assimilated" society in which everyone has the same color, educational background, economic status, national loyalty, and cultural viewpoint. But such a society would lack the healthy vitality and diversity of American pluralism.

COMMENT. I agree that the personal mental health of many individuals is strengthened if they have strong feelings of identification with some well-defined pluralist group within America's larger culture. But nothing about opening up the suburbs necessarily conflicts with this view. Economic integration at the job-access and public school scales is fully consistent with maintenance of separate neighborhoods by nationality or ethnic groups. Moreover, some members of every ethnic or nationality group prefer to live mixed among others rather than in self-segregated enclaves. They would benefit from the third scale of economic integration.

5. *Even if it is necessary to move many low-income households out of central cities in order to achieve the benefits described in chapter 5, having them settle in separate new communities created especially for the poor would be politically easier and more effective than trying to disperse them throughout each metropolitan area.* Therefore, opening up the suburbs should be achieved through "industrial new communities" on the periphery of existing metropolitan areas in which low- and moderate-income households would be concentrated. This would avoid all the political and social difficulties of trying to attain economic integration in already established or newly growing middle-class neighborhoods.[1]

COMMENT. Creating such new concentrations of the poor might soon generate suburban crisis ghettos, especially if both nonworking and working poor lived in these communities. Moreover, *all* the housing and most of the local services there would have to be directly subsidized by the federal government. It would probably be more difficult to get middle-class voters to support huge subsidies for new good quality communities from which they were excluded than to incorporate some subsidized housing in good quality communities in which they themselves also lived. Finally, development of viable new communities is an extremely difficult art not easily carried out on a large scale—especially when all middle- and upper-income households are excluded from potential residency.

6. *Opening up the suburbs requires continued large-scale building of new housing units on the edges of our metropolitan areas. But mere "uncontrolled sprawl" like that which has dominated past peripheral growth will cause a rapid deterioration of the general environment there.* We should try to avoid further spreading of uncoordinated land uses, excessive traffic congestion, declining open space, overloaded schools, and rising air and water pollution. Therefore the rate of peripheral urban development should be drastically slowed down, or even stopped. In particular, attempts to raise existing low population densities around the urban fringe by building more multifamily or cluster-type housing there should be strongly resisted. Yet those are precisely the types of housing most suitable for low- and moderate-income households. *Hence opening up the suburbs on any large scale is not compatible with preserving the minimum desirable quality of environment there.*

COMMENT. Strong concern by ecologists and environmentalists with maintaining the quality of the suburban environment has indeed fostered rapidly spreading hostility to further peripheral development. Nevertheless, in spite of falling fertility rates, the nation's metropolitan-area population is certain to rise significantly in the next few decades. In many large metropolitan areas, future natural increase alone will generate sizable additions to the local population. Where will these added households live? If they cannot move into peripheral new-growth areas, they must either occupy far-out "new communities" or live in older neighborhoods located closer in. But very few such "new communities" are being built, and raising their number would require large public subsidies. So it seems that any really stringent curtailment of paripheral growth in most metropolitan areas would inescapably generate a strong "back-pressure" upon existing older housing stocks. Densities, congestion, pollution, and lack of open space are already far worse in these more central neighborhoods than on the urban periphery, and these conditions would become even more aggravated if a real housing shortage reappeared. Yet that would happen if new peripheral development were choked off to less than that required to accommodate population growth. This would raise the rents and prices of older housing units in such central neighborhoods—thereby making low- and moderate-income households worse off. The result would be further deterioration in the already low quality environments in older neighborhoods in order to protect the already far superior quality environments in peripheral areas from suffering any decline.

Certainly it is proper for residents of low-density peripheral areas to seek better-planned growth than has occurred in the past. But it is neither reasonable nor just for them to be concerned solely with the quality of environments in their own areas while disregarding the negative impacts of that very concern upon the already worse environments elsewhere. That would be a form of pure "beggar-thy-neighbor," "now that we are here, nuts to everyone else" policy. Instead, the entire subject of controlling future urban development should be viewed from a metropolitan-area-wide perspective that takes the interests of *all* the area's residents into account—not just from the narrow parochial viewpoint of any one part of that area.

16 Making the Choice

This book has presented two main themes. One is that America's remaining urban poverty cannot be attacked effectively without reducing the spatial concentration of the poor. The second is that practical means of achieving this goal exist—means that would not seriously threaten the quality of life of the middle- and upper-income majority. However, adopting those means would require many members of that majority to make additional sacrifices in money, power, and degree of neighborhood dominance.

At present, I believe the American middle-class majority is overwhelmingly opposed to making these additional sacrifices. Although its members and leaders rhetorically express a desire to combat poverty and improve conditions in crisis ghettos, they show little willingness to bear the costs of doing so. In this chapter I wish to confront the basic question: why should middle- and upper-income Americans make any further sacrifices to combat poverty, particularly through economic integration? I will first discuss two related issues as background.

The Role of Opening Up the Suburbs in Combating Poverty

Some antipoverty policies could be adopted that would not involve specific efforts to open up the suburbs. These include adequate income maintenance, an economy geared to lower unemployment, and guaranteed job opportunities for every able worker. In my view, such policies are of higher priority in combating poverty than opening up the suburbs. But they would not eliminate the adverse and destructive conditions in many urban crisis ghettos. Concentrating the remaining multiproblem households in the worst urban housing, along with other low-income households, would still produce non-viable environments there—even if the absolute level of poverty were significantly raised. Therefore, a truly effective effort to improve the quality of life among the urban poor will require some opening up of the suburbs along the lines described in this book.

A unique advantage of this approach is that middle- and upper-income people, *personally*, are one of the potentially most effective resources for helping others escape poverty. Constant interaction of low-income children and adults with middle-class people, in constructive and positive settings, can powerfully aid the former. This has been demonstrated clearly in both education and employment. How well it might work regarding other aspects of behavior and value structure is not really known.

True, it is not easy to construct and maintain such personal interactions so that they are positive rather than demeaning to those who are upgrading. This could be a major challenge to the middle class to "become involved" in one of the most important activities in our society. I believe there is a widespread but largely untapped desire among middle-class and other Americans to do something personally in helping their fellow citizens in need. If so, many middle-class suburbanites might be willing to engage in such personal interaction in their own neighborhoods. And low-income households might be more receptive to such interaction within "normal" neighborhood institutions, such as schools and churches, than in obvious "cultural missionary" activities. Admittedly, I do not know if these suppositions will prove correct.

THE "SUFFERING MINORITY, SACRIFICING MAJORITY" DILEMMA

In the United States and a few other nations, the economic system has lifted most people out of poverty. The majority of families are not wealthy and still have myriad unsatisfied wants. Yet real poverty has become a malady of a relatively small numerical minority. In the United States in 1970, about 13 percent of the population was poor by the official definition. Thus, 87 percent of the population were *not* poor.

To mount an effective attack on poverty, this majority would have to pay significant costs. A very large portion of the poor cannot escape poverty unless others provide them with more money without receiving any direct benefits in return. Yet those who must sacrifice to end poverty are not themselves suffering from it. Because they comprise the vast majority of Americans, they cannot be compelled to make such sacrifices through political action if they strongly oppose doing so.

This political dilemma is central to many of our society's most serious domestic problems, including racism, hunger, crime, drug addiction, poor public schools, deteriorated housing, poor public transportation, and unemployment. Each directly affects millions of people—yet in every case they comprise only a small percentage of the total population. The remedies for each problem require members of the nonsuffering majority to pay significant costs from which they receive no direct benefits. In fact, they sometimes benefit from continuation of the problem (for example, high unemployment helps reduce inflation, thereby aiding the middle class). In our political system, it is difficult to exert political pressure upon members of a majority to make sacrifices they do not want to make. True, a well-financed and well-organized minority (such as oil producers) can bring pressure to bear to pass laws that actually penalize the majority. But the minority groups suffering from the above maladies have little money and are not well organized. As a result, they have been unable to muster sufficient political support to adopt effective remedies to their problems.

To retain the key virtues of democracy, we need to keep the principle of majority rule while somehow convincing the majority to be more responsive to the rights and welfare of various numerical minorities. There are three ways to do this. One is to form majority-sized coalitions of the suffering minorities described above plus some of the nonsuffering majority. This requires adopting policy responses to a problem that benefit both the minority suffering from it and part of the nonsuffering majority. The second way is to convince the majority to act by threatening it with dire consequences if it fails to do so. These two approaches appeal to the majority's self-interest. The third way is to appeal to the majority morally by emphasizing non-self-interest motives. All three ways are briefly explored in this chapter.

SELF-INTEREST REASONS

Improving the Productivity of the Employable Poor

Certain types of assistance to the employable poor would help them to become more productive workers in the future and perhaps to escape poverty. This would stimulate economic growth and raise the nation's total output; hence, it can be viewed as an investment. Furthermore, making low-skilled or unemployed workers more productive will reduce public costs of assisting them and of coping with related social maladies such as crime and disease.

My own admittedly crude calculations indicate that the *net* economic gains from upgrading the employable poor are probably not very large. They are not enough by themselves to stimulate the middle-class majority to bear the required costs for purely self-interest reasons. Yet those net gains *are* large enough to form an important part of some still larger set of incentives that might motivate the middle class to bear those costs.

Upgrading the Dependent Poor

Efforts to improve the employable poor consist of helping them become more productive within the free enterprise economy. But the free enterprise system contains no mechanisms for effectively serving persons who have no capital wealth and cannot produce marketable services, or who can only produce services with very low market values. Most of the poor are in precisely these categories. Hence the self-interest incentives causing producers to supply reasonably adequate goods and services for most people in our free enterprise system do not work regarding a majority of the poor.

Undoubtedly, that is a key reason why so many poor people and others concerned with their welfare are hostile to the free enterprise system. They recognize its indifference to the plight of those who are economically nonproductive by its own definitions of productivity. Moreover, the free enterprise system tends to disparage and demean these "nonproductive" persons psychologically as part of its maintaining strong work incentives among those who are potentially productive. Yet that system has been extremely successful at providing a majority of Americans with relatively high material standards of living.

Clearly, provision of adequate incomes for the "left-out" group must occur outside the "normal" operation of the free enterprise system. True, such provision may be of some economic benefit to those who pay for it. For example, removing the dependent poor from poverty might reduce disease, crime, and certain associated social costs. Yet I doubt that the purely economic cost savings would be as large as the dollar costs of lifting the dependent poor out of poverty.

Providing a Personal Insurance against Future Poverty

To what extent will middle-class citizens support additional antipoverty efforts as insurance against their becoming poor themselves? The three most likely causes of such poverty are unemployment, illness or disability, and old age.

The vast majority of middle-class households—probably over 95 percent—are not suffering from unemployment. Most experience it so rarely that they do not fear becoming poor because of lack of a job. The two most likely causes of poverty for them are illness or injury preventing them from working and old age. The strength of middle-class sentiment in regard to these causes is shown by the adoption of Medicare and Medicaid programs, their rapid funding growth, continual increases in Social Security coverage and benefit levels, and the relative popularity of public housing for the elderly. Thus this form of self-interest is indeed likely to motivate further support for antipoverty efforts among the middle class. But it is not likely to include accepting much dispersal of poor persons into middle-income neighborhoods—except for the elderly. Yet it is younger households—especially those containing employable members or schoolchildren—who most need the job opportunities and improved schooling available in the suburbs.

Protecting against Possible Violence and Disruption

During the racial disorders of 1965 through 1968, many people argued that massive public spending to improve urban ghettos was necessary to prevent disastrous future violence. Black radicals threatened to "burn down America's cities" if major improvements were not made in the status and opportunities of blacks. Later, student radicals threatened to initiate large-scale urban guerrilla warfare. The desire to avoid future violence might provide a self-interest motive for the middle class to combat poverty more effectively.

If this reasoning is taken to mean that the middle class *must* enact massive additional programs against urban poverty or else face violent domestic revolutionary efforts that will disrupt peaceful suburban life, I believe it is false. If it is taken to mean that failure to combat urban poverty more effectively will perpetuate high urban crime rates, could lead to some large-scale disorders, and might reduce individual civil rights, then I believe it is true.

The civil disorders in black ghettos that began about 1965 were disturbing and destructive. So were student riots and urban bombings a few years later. Yet none of these phenomena came close to "burning down" even one city. In fact, *each* of several recent hurricanes caused more property damage than *all* civil disturbances since 1960 combined. Moreover, more people are killed and injured in automobile accidents on any *one* average holiday weekend than in *all* civil disorders since 1960 combined. I cite these comparisons not to minimize the disturbing nature of civil disorders but to place them in a reasonable perspective.

Considering economic factors alone, it would be far cheaper to repress future large-scale urban violence through police and military action than to pay for effective programs against remaining urban poverty. This might require abrogating the civil rights of many citizens deplorably. Yet it could be done with little other inconvenience to the middle class.

Urban crime will be far harder to repress and will cause much more difficulty for middle-class citizens. Crime rates have been rising sharply throughout the nation during the past few years, even in suburban areas. The relationship between high crime rates and poverty is ambiguous. In the short run, it is not clear whether effective programs attacking urban poverty would cause urban crime rates to rise, fall, or remain the same. The answer depends greatly upon whether these programs were accompanied by major reforms in the existing system of criminal justice, as discussed earlier. Yet *in the long run,* central-city blighted areas will grow if we fail to reduce urban poverty and disperse the urban poor more effectively. The portions of each metropolitan area considered unsafe will therefore expand, too. Avoiding these outcomes provides a strong self-interest motive for middle-class citizens to support more effective antipoverty efforts. Yet such efforts may not produce immediate reductions in crime rates.

Obtaining Specific Benefits

Certain groups would benefit directly and immediately from effective dispersal policies. Therefore, they are potential sources of political support for such policies. They include:

1. *Suburban employers—especially industrialists.* This group needs more low- and moderate-income workers living close to their places of business.
2. *Suburban labor unions and workers.* Many members of this group have great difficulty finding appropriate housing near their jobs.
3. *Home-builders.* These entrepreneurs would benefit from subsidy programs stimulating the creation of new suburban housing for low- and moderate-income households.
4. *Building trades workers.* These workers would benefit for the same reason as home-builders.
5. *Central-city politicians and government officials.* The fiscal

and other problems of many central cities would be eased if there were significant dispersal of the poor to suburban areas.

6. *Lower middle-class central-city homeowners.* If there is no dispersal of poor central-city households to the suburbs, areas within central cities occupied by such households will expand. This will cause greater transition of existing lower middle-class neighborhoods to low-income occupancy than would occur if dispersal were effective.

7. *Owners of central-city business and other property.* Further expansion of low-income areas within large central cities would weaken the economies of those cities.

8. *Low- and moderate-income central-city households.* Dispersal would offer these households opportunities to live in better suburban environments and help reduce poverty concentrations where they now live.

9. *Low- and moderate-income suburban households.* Construction of more suburban housing for this income group would expand the housing choices available to its members who already reside in the suburbs.

All these groups combined do not comprise a majority in most metropolitan areas. Yet they could muster great political strength if they organized effectively behind key dispersal policies.

NON-SELF-INTEREST REASONS

Self-interest is usually the most powerful motive behind political action in a democracy, but altruistic motives can also be important. There are two main non-self-interest reasons why the middle class should make further efforts to attack remaining urban poverty, especially by opening up the suburbs.

Counteracting Social Injustice

Social justice means providing every citizen with whatever is properly due to him or her. It may be due in return for specific past or present contributions to society or because of rights granted to every citizen by society. Thus, providing justice to the poor is not charity, which goes beyond what is due. Rather, it is a requirement of any social order run with integrity.

Exactly how much assistance the urban poor have a right to demand from others is extremely hard to determine. But there are two powerful reasons to believe they have a right to more assistance than they are now receiving.

For one thing, our society has deliberately designed its urban development process so that it worsens the living conditions of the urban poor in order to benefit those who are more affluent, as described in chapter 1. This process also separates many unemployed but potentially employable workers from the areas where most new job opportunities are being created and separates low-income children from the best educational facilities. Justice therefore requires some action to counteract these adverse impacts upon many non-elderly low-income households. The middle class pays for significant antipoverty assistance via welfare programs and other aids. But few—if any—of these help to counteract the specific injuries inflicted by concentrating poverty in crisis ghettos and denying many of the poor access to suburban jobs and amenities.

In addition, every modern industrialized society systematically consigns a certain percentage of its members to poverty for reasons beyond their control. This is especially evident in free enterprise economies, where markets determine who gets what. Few of the resulting poor have chosen their condition voluntarily. Most are unable to produce services valued by the economy for reasons wholly beyond their own control. The economic arrangements that keep them from receiving "minimally acceptable" incomes are man-made practices continued by society because they benefit the majority of citizens. Is it "just" to compel some citizens to suffer economic deprivation in order to maintain social arrangements that benefit the rest?

In societies that are relatively poor as a whole, the answer might be "yes." Because of their low total outputs, they cannot afford to provide a "minimally acceptable" standard of living to economically nonproductive citizens. But this is hardly the case in the United States today. Is it therefore socially just to allow 13 percent of all Americans to live in poverty? I believe a reasonable—though not unequivocal—argument can be made that social justice requires the complete elimination of remaining poverty in the United States, as "poverty" is now officially defined.

Naturally this argument seems especially forceful to the poor. It is difficult for them to understand why social justice does not require providing for their minimal economic needs when the nation can afford public funding for exploration of the moon, subsidies for wealthy oil producers, agricultural price supports that mainly aid large-scale farmers but *raise* food prices to poor consumers, tax shelters for wealthy investors in housing, higher education for affluent young people, and so on.

The Unity of Each Metropolitan Area, the Nation, and the World

The final reason for further efforts to attack poverty combines two types of transcendence: spiritual and ecological. Both embody the belief that the human race is a single unity or brotherhood, so the welfare of each person is related to the welfare of all others. Spiritually, this idea transcends both material questions and social justice. A central doctrine in all religions, it implies that the relatively affluent have a strong moral obligation to make greater efforts to aid others still suffering from material deprivation.

Exactly how far the affluent should go toward assisting the deprived is ambiguous. Who should be considered part of the group that matters to the affluent? Should it be just the family, or the local community, or the whole metropolitan area, or the state, or the entire nation, or all of mankind? In this book, I have contended that every American has a primary obligation toward all the residents of his or her own metropolitan area and an almost equal obligation toward all other Americans. How will the American middle class decide for whom it bears some moral responsibility? The answer depends upon how seriously its members take the ethical and religious values they profess, including the traditional American values of equal opportunity and social justice for all. What does the principle, "Love thy neighbor as thyself," really mean to us? The need to open up the suburbs challenges us to answer this question by at least helping "our own" poor escape their poverty in recognition of our unity with them.

Although the unity of mankind has been mainly a *spiritual* principle throughout human history, it is now coming to be recognized as a *material* principle too. Rising levels of pollution throughout the world plus impending shortages of certain materials and energy sources make us realize more concretely how the quality of life of every individual on earth is influenced by the behavior of all other human beings. Yet it will be a long time before our present failure to recognize the ecological unity of mankind produces serious disasters. In fact, it will be so long that not many people are likely to bear present sacrifices to avoid those disasters. In contrast, serious problems have already arisen from our failure to reduce concentrated poverty in our urban areas. This fact should help Americans recognize and respond to the unity of our metropolitan areas much faster than to the unity of the entire world.

Is Self-Interest Enough?

Many observers believe that the public in a democracy is rarely activated by anything other than its own perceived self-interest. They argue that only self-interest reasons can exert much influence upon the middle class to increase its antipoverty efforts—or to open up the suburbs.

In my opinion, exclusive reliance upon self-interest motivation will not accomplish either of these goals. As I have tried to point out above, the self-interest reasons why the middle class should *further* attack poverty are just not very powerful—particularly since we already support many poverty-alleviating policies. We have gone about as far as we are likely to go toward attacking poverty if we rely solely upon self-interest arguments to increase such attacks. In fact, I believe our progress to this point already results in part from non-self-interest motives. But prevailing political sentiments indicate a widespread desire to halt further income redistribution in favor of using more public policies to aid the middle class. To some extent, I believe this is a quasi-cyclical phenomenon. Current sentiments represent a reaction to the overly optimistic antipoverty efforts of the late 1960's. The pendulum may swing back toward stronger support for antipoverty actions in the future. Yet even then, I doubt that rational self-interest alone can ever produce strong enough antipoverty efforts to come close to eliminating remaining poverty in the United States.

To achieve that objective requires going beyond self-interest and also acting to a significant extent out of feelings of human solidarity, or brotherhood, or compassion, or similar forms of what is really love of others. In this respect, our national life is quite analogous to family life. No family whose members were motivated solely by rational self-interest would ever achieve very profound harmony, equality, or mutual self-development among its members. Life in such a family would fall far short of achieving its maximum human potential either as a whole or for the individual members. At least some family members —especially the most powerful and initially most competent— the parents—must be willing to make significant self-sacrifices motivated by love for the other members to achieve that maximum human potential. Similarly, I believe achieving the best potential quality of life in our democratic society would require many citizens—especially among the middle-class majority—to willingly make significant sacrifices to benefit others out of idealism, altruism, or love—not just self-interest.

The above paragraph is presented as a scientific conclusion, not a personal value judgment. Although it may sound moralistic, it expresses my objective description of how our society—or any other—really works, not of how it should work. To put it as a scientific hypothesis, if a society's dominant groups are not significantly motivated by non-self-interest factors, the society cannot attain the best quality of life potentially available to it—by almost anyone's definition of "best quality of life." Admittedly, I cannot confirm this conclusion by arraying masses of empirical data. Nevertheless I believe it is profoundly important in understanding the issues in this book. It implies that we are unlikely to come close to eliminating poverty and might not significantly open up the suburbs unless there is some way to influence the middle class to act from non-self-interest motives, as well as in pursuit of its own interests.

Can this be done? I hope so, but I really do not know. It surely cannot be done unless key leaders in our society seeking to end poverty recognize the need to appeal to motives beyond self-interest and are willing to make such appeals. This view is often stated in Fourth of July oratory, but it is not very popular among social scientists or American social observers generally—including those most strongly committed to ending poverty. Insofar as they are willing to deal with human motives at all, they prefer to concentrate upon those clearly related to self-interest. Therefore, when they seek to achieve a certain policy goal—such as ending poverty—they focus upon appealing to the self-interest motives supporting that objective. This "tough-minded" approach seems more realistic and less open to charges of sentimentality than the conclusions I have stated above. Moreover, empirical evidence supporting the strength of self-interest motives is easier to find than that supporting the strength of non-self-interest motives.

But I am not arguing that non-self-interest motives are in fact strong at present—or ever will be. Rather, I contend that *until* they are at least significant and are effectively evoked along with self-interest motives, America will never eliminate its remaining domestic poverty, and might not open up the suburbs.

MAKING THE CHOICE

In theory, America can choose among many patterns of future urban development. In reality, our most important choice is between continuing the present trickle-down process and shifting to some type of economic integration strategy. All the power and inertia of established social, economic, and political forces and institutions are on the side of continuing trickle-down urban development. In contrast, opening up the suburbs would require major changes in these forces and institutions. Clearly, it is much easier to choose a continuation of the *status quo*—and that is precisely what we are doing.

If we do not alter this implicit choice, we will systematically exclude the lower-income half of our population from sharing in the economic opportunities created by future suburban growth. The suburbs are where the economic action is and will continue to be. They will experience tremendous growth in population, housing, jobs, urban facilities, and relatively high quality environments. But most Americans—and all relatively poor ones—will fail to share in that growth unless we break away from the existing trickle-down pattern of development to at least some extent.

Continuing that process unaltered will also condemn large parts of our older central cities to collapse physically, economically, and humanly. We have recently encountered a new phenomenon in American life in these areas: the abandonment of housing units, buildings, even whole neighborhoods. Many are desolate, as though struck by air raids. Most plans to redevelop these areas will remain fanciful unless the concentration of low-income households in central cities is reduced. No households, business firms, or even sensible governments will sink capital into the destructive environments endemic to concentrated poverty areas. Yet greatly improving those environments is impossible unless that concentration is reduced through the movement of some low- and moderate-income households to suburban areas.

Opening up the suburbs will not be easy. It requires two basic shifts in past practices that most Americans have continually refused to make. The first is accepting the idea that urban development in each metropolitan area ought to proceed in accordance with a single overall strategy and then creating institutions to carry out such a strategy. This does not necessarily mean adopting metropolitan government. But it does mean recognizing the interdependence of all metropolitan-area residents in a politically meaningful way. The second basic shift is acceptance by middle-class Americans of some low- and moderate-income neighbors in suburban communities, in places of employment, in schools, and sometimes on the same block. I believe this can be done without significantly reducing the quality of life in middle-class neighborhoods. Furthermore, it would create new opportunities for more meaningful interactions among economic groups that could enrich American culture.

Choosing to open up the suburbs is not a single event but a long-term process. Like most other fundamental social and economic issues in our modern democracy, this one cannot be "resolved" by arrival at some well-defined end-state or social outcome. There are too many conflicting viewpoints on almost every major issue. The best we can do is to obtain preponderant agreement about some basic *direction* in which social policy ought to move from where we are now. That would be enough to start appropriate policies. Once they are launched, they must be altered by continual feedback.

Most Americans—including the vast majority of suburbanites—do not now want to move in the direction of opening up the suburbs. They are benefiting from the trickle-down process and they do not want to bear the costs of changing it. Therefore, as an objective analyst, I forecast that our society is not likely to make the policy choice advocated in this book.

Yet I believe it is the right choice for America. It best serves the nation's long-run self-interest and most closely conforms to our highest spiritual and moral principles. Continuing the trickle-down process unaltered will weaken the nation in the long run. It will also demonstrate a cynical disregard for elementary social justice and for long established American values. Up to now, we have partly concealed these results from ourselves because few people have understood the true implications of our urban development process. I hope this book will help reduce or eliminate that ignorance. Insofar as it does, it will remove our excuse for failing to do what is right.

In this modern world of astoundingly rapid change, what appears implausible today often becomes reality tomorrow. I hope I have made opening up the suburbs seem a more plausible and desirable course for America's future urban development and thereby helped make it more likely to happen.

Appendix

Suburbs have a lower proportion of relatively low-income families than central cities. The bar graph below shows the percentage of families with 1969 incomes under $5,000.

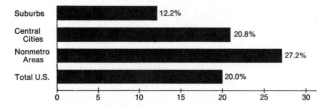

Suburbs have a higher proportion of relatively high-income families than central cities. The bar graph below shows the percentage of families with 1969 incomes $15,000 and over.

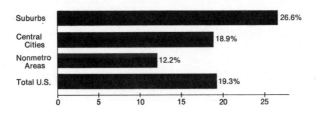

Suburbs have a lower number and proportion of persons with incomes below officially defined "poverty levels" than

* The first two graphs are from U.S. Bureau of the Census, *Demographic, Economic, and Revenue Trends for Major Central Cities* (special tabulations prepared for a briefing with Secretary George Romney of the Department of Housing and Urban Development, Sept. 9, 1971), p. 2. The third is from Bureau of the Census, *Current Population Reports: Consumer Income*, ser. P-60, no. 77, May 7, 1971, p. 6.

central cities. The bar graph below shows persons with 1970 incomes below official poverty levels.

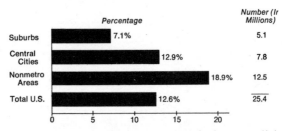

For all the above indicators, central-city conditions are about the same as those in the nation as a whole, on the average; whereas nonmetropolitan areas are clearly the poorest parts of the nation.

PERCENTAGE CHANGES IN OCCUPIED HOUSING UNITS AND POPULATION BY GEOGRAPHIC AREAS FOR THE ENTIRE NATION, 1960–70 *

In all geographic areas, the inventory of occupied housing units grew more (in percentage) than total population. This means that housing conditions improved in all areas, at least as far as the supply available to meet demand was concerned. The bar graph below shows the percentage increase, 1960–70, in occupied housing inventory (black) and total population (gray).

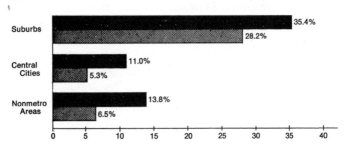

* Bureau of the Census, *Statistical Abstract of the United States, 1972*, 93d ed. (Washington, D.C., 1972), pp. 16, 689.

However, the *ratio* of percentage growth in occupied housing to percentage growth in population was much larger in central cities and nonmetropolitan areas than in suburbs. This means the degree of improvement in housing conditions was greater in those other areas than in suburbs, in relation to population growth. The bar graph shows the ratio of percentage increase in occupied housing inventory to percentage increase in population, 1960–70.

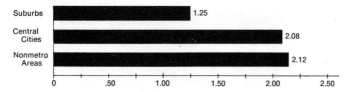

SUBURBAN PERCENTAGE SHARES OF TOTAL HOUSING CONSTRUCTION ACTIVITY AND CHANGES IN RELATED VARIABLES FOR TEN METROPOLITAN AREAS, 1960–70 *

The data represented in the bar graphs are for the ten metropolitan areas with the largest absolute population increases from 1960 to 1970: Los Angeles/Long Beach, Washington, New York, Orange County, California, Chicago, Houston, Philadelphia, San Francisco/Oakland, Dallas, and San Jose. *Suburban share* means percentage of variable change occurring in suburbs, considering total change within the metropolitan area as equal to 100 percent.

In these ten metropolitan areas taken together, the suburban share of new housing construction was larger than the suburban share of total 1970 population. So suburbs experienced more new housing construction than central cities both absolutely and in relation to total population.

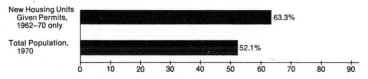

* Special tabulations of Bureau of the Census Building Permit reports by Real Estate Research Corporation, plus *Statistical Abstract, 1972.*

But in the same ten areas, the suburban share of new housing construction was *smaller* than the suburban shares of either population growth or net change in existing housing inventory from 1960–70.

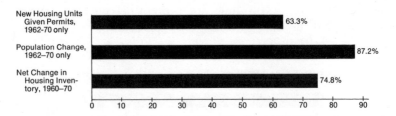

Thus, in these areas, expansion of the housing supply relative to added population needs during the 1960s was far greater in central cities than in suburbs—even though the suburbs experienced more new housing construction.

HOUSING DIFFERENCES BETWEEN SUBURBS AND CENTRAL CITIES, 1970 *

Owner-occupied housing is more expensive in suburbs than in central cities, on the average. The median value of single-family, owner-occupied units was 21.2 percent higher in suburbs in 1970. The bar graph shows median values of single-family owner-occupied homes.

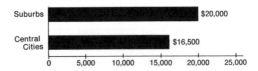

Rental housing is also more expensive in suburbs than in central cities, on the average. The median rent paid was 24.2 percent higher in suburbs in 1970. The bar graph shows monthly median rent paid in non-owner-occupied housing units.

* The first two graphs are from Bureau of the Census, *1970 Census of Population and Housing*. The third is from *Statistical Abstract, 1972*, p. 689.

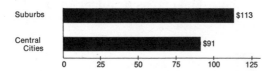

The percentage of owner occupancy in all occupied units is higher in suburbs than in central cities for major ethnic groups. The bar graph shows percentage of owner-occupied units among whites (black) and blacks and other races (gray) by areas.

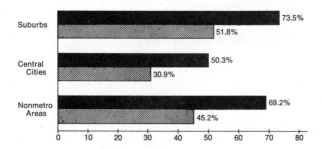

Housing Availability to Low-Income Households in Suburbs and Central Cities, 1970 *

The percentage of total housing inventory available to low-income households in 1970 was rather low in both central cities and suburbs but much higher in central cities. Low-income households are those with incomes about $4,000 or less, and housing that they could pay for is theoretically available to them.

Owner-occupied homes valued at under $12,500 cost no more than slightly over three times the annual income of households with $4,000 per year. The percentages of owner-occupied units in all value categories below this level are shown for suburbs (black) and central cities (gray) in the graph below. Central cities have a higher percentage of owner-occu-

* Bureau of the Census, *1970 Census of Population and Housing.*

pied homes than do suburbs in all of these categories and almost twice as high a percentage for all combined.

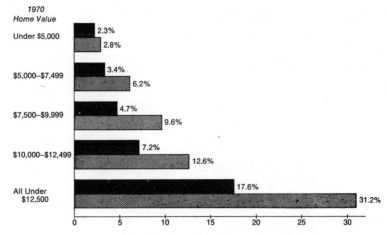

Rental units priced at under $80 per month would absorb less than 25 percent of the income of households receiving $4,000 per year. The percentages of rental units in all rent categories below this level are shown for suburbs (black) and central cities (gray) in the graph below. Again, central cities have higher fractions in all categories and about twice as high a total fraction for all combined.

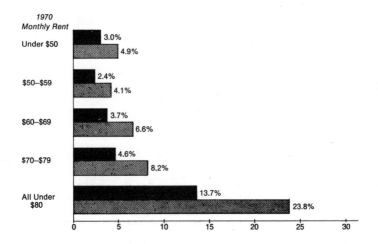

CONCENTRATION OF BLACK AMERICANS IN CENTRAL CITIES*

In 1970 all central cities combined had a much higher percentage of black residents in their total population than all suburbs combined. Both the number and percentage had also risen much more in central cities than in suburbs since 1950. The bar graph below shows the percentage of blacks in total population in 1950 (black) and in 1970 (gray) and the number of blacks in each area in the same years.

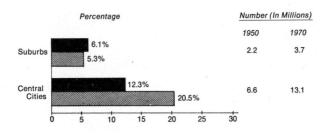

As a result of the above developments, more than half of the entire black population of the United States lived in central cities in 1970. In contrast, the white population was more concentrated in the suburbs than in any other geographic area. The bar graph shows the percentage of total U.S. population of blacks (black) and whites (gray) residing in various geographic areas in 1970.

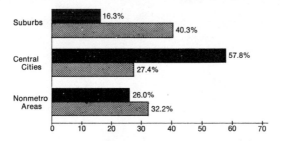

In spite of the concentration of American blacks in central cities, it should be remembered that the vast majority of all

* *Statistical Abstract, 1972*, pp. 16, 21–23.

central cities are predominantly white in ethnic composition. Among the 153 cities with over 100,000 residents in 1970, only four had black majorities and seven others had from 40 to 50 percent blacks in their total populations.

Cities with Black Majorities in 1970	*Cities with Populations 40–50% Black in 1970*
Atlanta	Baltimore
Gary	Birmingham
Newark	Detroit
Washington, D.C.	New Orleans
	Richmond
	Saint Louis
	Savannah

GEOGRAPHIC LOCATION OF WHITE AND BLACK POPULATION GROWTH, 1960–70 *

A very high proportion of all the growth in the American black population took place in central cities from 1960 to 1970. Suburbs experienced some share of this growth, but nonmetropolitan areas actually lost black population through out-migration—mainly to central cities. The graph shows the percentage of total U.S. growth in black population occurring in each type of area in these years.

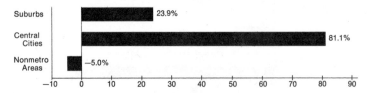

In contrast, the largest proportion of all the growth in the American white population occurred in suburbs from 1960 to 1970. Central cities actually lost a slight amount of white population because of massive white out-migration to suburbs during this period. The graph shows the percentage of total

* *Statistical Abstract, 1972*, p. 16.

U.S. growth in white population occurring in each type of area in these years.

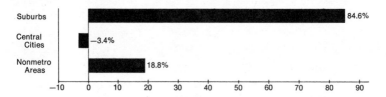

Because of the concentrated growth of black population in central cities, a high fraction of total central-city population growth from 1960 to 1970 consisted of increases in black population. Although these cities combined actually lost white population, other ethnic groups in them expanded. In contrast, suburban population growth as a whole was overwhelmingly white in this same period. The graph shows the percentage of total population growth in each type of area consisting of increases in black population in these years.

Table A.1
U.S. Population by Geographic Areas, 1900–70
(In millions of persons)

Year	Total Co-terminous U.S.	All Metropolitan Areas	All Central Cities	All Suburbs	All Non-metropolitan Areas
1900	75.995	31.836	19.786	12.051	44.159
1910	91.972	42.012	27.122	14.890	49.960
1920	105.711	52.508	34.641	17.866	53.203
1930	122.775	66.712	43.070	23.642	56.063
1940	131.669	72.576	45.473	27.103	59.093
1950	150.697	88.964	52.138	36.826	61.733
1960	178.464	112.385	57.710	54.675	66.079
	(179.323)	(170.159)	(60.630)	(59.529)	(59.164)
1970	203.166	140.156	63.825	76.331	63.010

SOURCE: U.S. Bureau of the Census

NOTES: Data for 1900 through 1960 are for the 212 areas classified as metropolitan areas by the Census Bureau in 1960. Data for 1970 are for the 230 areas classified as metropolitan areas by the Census Bureau in 1970. For convenience, the 1960 population data for these 230 areas are shown in parentheses below the 1960 data for 212 areas.

The 1970 total U.S. population is from a slightly different series than the 1960 total. The latter is comparable to 1900 through 1950 data. Hence a second 1960 total is shown in parentheses beneath the first. This second number is comparable to the 1970 total.

Table A.2
Percentage Shares of Total U.S. Population
by Geographic Areas, 1900–70

Year	All Metropolitan Areas	All Central Cities	All Suburbs	All Nonmetropolitan Areas
1900	41.9	26.0	15.9	58.1
1910	45.7	29.5	16.2	54.3
1920	49.7	32.8	16.9	50.3
1930	54.3	35.1	19.2	45.7
1940	55.1	34.5	20.6	44.9
1950	59.0	34.6	24.4	41.0
1960 (212 areas)	63.0	32.3	30.7	37.0
1960 (230 areas)	67.0	33.8	33.2	33.0
1970	69.0	31.4	37.6	31.0

SOURCE: Same as for table A.1, except two separate tabulations are shown here for differing 1960 definitions of metropolitan areas.

Table A.3
U.S. Population Growth by Geographic Areas, 1900–70
(In millions of persons and in percentages)

Decade	Total Co-terminous U.S.	All Met-ropolitan Areas	All Central Cities	All Suburbs	All Non-metropolitan Areas
1900–10	15.978 (21.0%)	10.176 (32.0%)	7.337 (37.1%)	2.839 (23.6%)	5.801 (13.1%)
1910–20	13.738 (14.9%)	10.496 (26.1%)	7.519 (27.7%)	2.977 (20.0%)	3.243 (6.5%)
1920–30	17.064 (16.1%)	14.204 (27.1%)	8.428 (24.3%)	5.776 (32.3%)	2.860 (5.4%)
1930–40	8.894 (7.2%)	5.864 (8.8%)	2.403 (5.6%)	3.461 (14.6%)	3.030 (5.4%)
1940–50	19.028 (14.4%)	16.388 (22.6%)	6.664 (14.6%)	9.723 (35.9%)	2.640 (4.5%)
1950–60	27.767 (18.4%)	23.421 (26.3%)	5.573 (10.7%)	17.848 (48.5%)	4.346 (7.0%)
1960–70	23.842 (13.3%)	19.997 (16.6%)	3.194 (5.3%)	16.803 (28.2%)	3.845 (6.5%)

NOTE: Data derived from table A.1; source same as for that table. Data for 1960–70 compare figures for 230 areas classified as metropolitan in 1970. All percentages use 1960 figures as base.

Table A.4
Percentage of Total Metropolitan-Area
Population Growth Occurring in
Central Cities and Suburbs

Decade	Central Cities	Suburbs
1900–10	72.1	27.9
1910–20	71.6	28.4
1920–30	59.3	40.7
1930–40	40.8	59.2
1940–50	40.7	59.3
1950–60	23.8	76.2
1960–70	16.0	84.0

SOURCE: U.S. Bureau of the Census
NOTE: 212 metropolitan areas for all periods
through 1950–60; 230 areas for 1960–70.

Table A.5
Change in Employed Civilians Age 14 and Over
by Place of Worker Residence, 1960–70
(Numbers in thousands)

Area of Worker Residence	Male		Female		Total	
	Number	Per-centage	Number	Per-centage	Number	Per-centage
Central Cities	−284	−2.0	+1,451	+17.5	+1,167	+5.1
Suburbs	+4,674	+35.4	+4,419	+74.4	+9,093	+47.5
Metropolitan Areas	+4,390	+16.0	+5,870	+41.2	+10,260	+24.6
Nonmetropolitan Areas	+2,118	+17.1	+3,141	+48.7	+5,259	+27.8
Total U.S.	+6,508	+16.3	+9.011	+43.6	+15,519	+25.6

SOURCE: U.S., Congress, Senate, *Congressional Record*, vol. 117, no. 36, pp. 5-3250-51 (March 16, 1971).

Notes

PREFACE

1   Data on poverty are from Bureau of the Census, *Current Population Reports: Consumer Income*, ser. P-60, no. 77, May 7, 1971. Data on median incomes are from Bureau of the Census, *Current Population Reports: Consumer Income*, ser. P-60, no. 78, May 20, 1971.
2   Communities that are considered *suburbs* by this definition range in population from a few hundred to over 80,000, in land-use composition from entirely residential to almost entirely industrial with nearly all possible mixtures in between, and in distance from the central city from immediate adjacency to over a hundred miles away. A similar diversity also exists among central cities.

CHAPTER 1

1   Mobile homes are lower in quality than conventionally built houses because they are smaller, less durably constructed, have fewer amenities, and normally occupy much less land per unit. However I do not mean to imply that mobile homes are undesirable dwelling units or of unacceptably low quality. On the contrary, most mobile homes provide excellent accommodations well-suited to the desires and economic capabilities of their occupants.
2   U.S. Bureau of the Census, *Construction Reports: Characteristics of New One-Family Homes* (ser. C25-71-13).
3   These statistics are from U.S. Bureau of the Census, *Demographic, Economic, and Revenue Trends for Major Central Cities*, a special tabulation prepared in September 1971 for a briefing with Secretary George Romney of the Department of Housing and Urban Development, September 9, 1971.
4   Data are taken from information supplied by the Cook County Department of Public Assistance for an earlier year and extrapolated to the number of persons on welfare in April 1971.

5   Perry Prentice has defended the trickle-down process in general
by pointing to its success in the market for automobiles, where
used cars provide relatively inexpensive transportation for low-
income households. In fact, I favor retention of the trickle-down
process as the major way of supplying housing to most American
households of all income groups, as noted in the text. But the way
that process now works generates undesirable spatial concentration of very poor households in a manner that has no counterpart
in automobile markets. It is that excessive *concentration* of poverty
—not the basic idea of allowing housing to "trickle-down," to at
least some extent—that I believe must be changed if we are to
make any significant progress toward "solving" many current
urban problems.

CHAPTER 2

1   Main sources for the data used in chap. 2 include U.S. Bureau of
the Census, *Demographic, Economic, and Revenue Trends for Major
Central Cities* (Romney Briefing Document); U.S. Bureau of the
Census, *Current Population Reports: Current Income*, ser. P-60, no. 77,
May 7, 1971; statement of Dr. George H. Brown, director of the
Bureau of the Census, before the U.S. Commission on Civil
Rights, Washington, D.C., June 14, 1971 (hearings on barriers to
minority suburban access); U.S. Bureau of the Census, *Statistical
Abstract of the United States, 1971*, 92d ed. (Washington, D.C., 1971)
(Table 14, Population by Residence and Race, p. 16); Anthony
Downs, *Who Are the Urban Poor?*, Committee for Economic
Development, Supplementary Paper no. 26, rev. ed. (New York,
1970); U.S. Bureau of the Census, news release CB71–72,
February 10, 1971, with accompanying tables; Advisory Com-
mission on Intergovernmental Relations, *Fiscal Balance in the
American Federal System*, vol. 2, *Metropolitan Fiscal Disparities* (Wash-
ington: U.S. Government Printing Office, 1967).

CHAPTER 3

1   Census Bureau figures concerning the 1970 metropolitan-area
breakdown of population have varied slightly from time to time
since preliminary data from the 1970 census began appearing.
The 1970 figures cited in this paragraph and in the tables in the

rest of chap. 3 and in the Appendix were taken from some of the Census Bureau's earlier releases. The bureau has modified these figures somewhat since then—mainly by reducing the suburban population and raising the nonmetropolitan population slightly, in both cases by less than 800,000 persons. Rather than revising all the tables in this chapter, I have used the earlier data. The small resulting percentage variations from those derivable from later data have no significant impact upon any of the reasoning or conclusions in this book.

2   Tables A.1–A.5 in the Appendix present the data from which this chapter was drawn.

3   See the article by Jack Rosenthal in the *New York Times*, October 15, 1972, pp. 1, 58. All the figures in this section were taken from Rosenthal's excellent analysis of employment trends within the 15 largest metropolitan areas.

4   Two of the leading proponents of this view are Dr. George Brown, former director of the Census Bureau, and Dr. George Sternlieb of Rutgers University. See especially Sternlieb's "The City as Sandbox," *Public Interest*, no. 25 (Fall 1971), pp. 14–21.

CHAPTER 4

1   The concentration of metropolitan-area unemployment in low-income, central-city neighborhoods has been documented by many previous empirical studies; therefore no detailed evidence is required here. See especially the *Report of the National Advisory Commission on Civil Disorders* (Washington: Government Printing Office, 1968), chap. 7.

2   Edward Banfield is a leading proponent of this view, as set forth in his book, *The Unheavenly City* (Boston: Little, Brown and Co., 1968), especially chaps. 3 and 10. Oscar Lewis has also argued that a "culture of poverty" exists; see for example *La Vida* (New York: Random House, 1965).

3   Lee Rainwater is the advocate of this view whose work has influenced me most strongly. A short summary of his approach can be found in *Work, Well-Being and Family Life*, Joint Center for Urban Studies, Working Paper no. 15 (Cambridge, Mass., June 1972). Another work reflecting a similar perspective is Elliot Liebow, *Tally's Corner* (Boston: Little, Brown and Co., 1967).

4   James S. Coleman et al., *Equality of Educational Opportunity* (Washington: U.S. Office of Education, 1966).

5   The most thorough critique I know of is Frederick Mosteller and Daniel P. Moynihan, eds., *On Equality of Educational Opportunity* (New York: Vintage Books, 1972). This volume contains a series of thoughtful essays on the Coleman report by a variety of authors who subjected the original data to thorough reanalysis.

6   Christopher Jencks, with Marshall Smith, Henry Acland, Mary Jo Bane, David Cohen, Herbert Gintis, Barbara Heyns, and Stephan Michelson, *Inequality: A Reassessment of the Effect of Family and Schooling in America* (New York, Basic Books, 1972).

7   A detailed defense of this conclusion is set forth in "Moving Toward Realistic Housing Goals," chap. 4 of my *Urban Problems and Prospects* (Chicago: Markham Publishing Co., 1970).

8   National Commission on Urban Problems, *Building the American City* (New York: Frederick Praeger, 1969). The total number of substandard units in 1960 is taken from p. 70 and the percentage breakdown by areas from p. 74.

9   Advisory Commission on Intergovernmental Relations, *Metropolitan Fiscal Disparities*, pp. 4–7.

10 *Report of the National Advisory Commission on Civil Disorders*, pp. 225–26.

11 Downs, *Who Are the Urban Poor?* p. 14.

CHAPTER 5

1   John D. Heinberg, *The Transfer Cost of a Housing Allowance: Conceptual Issues and Benefit Patterns* (Washington: Urban Institute, 1971).

2   An American household is officially considered poor if 33 percent of its income (the fraction society believes it "should be able to afford" for food) is not enough to buy the bare subsistence diet that the Department of Agriculture has defined as "minimally acceptable." In 1971, the cost of such a diet for a household of four was about $1,300 per year—or 30 cents per meal per person. Hence any four-person household with a 1971 income below about $3,900 per year was considered poor, because 33 percent of its income would not pay for that diet. One version of the Family Assistance Plan proposed in 1971 would have raised incomes of

all four-person households to a minimum of about $2,400, or less than two-thirds of the official "food poverty level" for such households. Yet Congress failed to adopt even this standard. If Congress believes ending food poverty is too expensive, it will surely be unwilling to support the much larger total subsidies required to end housing poverty.

3   Statistics in the following paragraphs were taken from National Commission on Urban Problems, *Building the American City*, p. 3.

4   Estimates of housing-unit sizes in Moscow, Great Britain, and Sweden are based upon data I gathered in those areas while on a tour of new cities in Europe in 1969. Estimates used later for Hong Kong are based upon data obtained in that city by Morris A. Lieberman in 1972.

5   U.S. Bureau of the Census, *1970 Census of Population and Housing*.

6   Data used for the calculations in this paragraph are from several sources. Expenditure data are from U.S. Bureau of the Census, *Statistical Abstract of the United States, 1971*.

In 1970, the average expenditure per public elementary and secondary pupil in the United States was $783. About 53 percent of this amount, or $415, was raised from local revenue sources (rather than state or federal aid). A typical effective tax rate for *all* real property taxes levied in a given area is 2.5 percent of actual market value. About 45 percent of local property taxes are used for schools on the average; so it is reasonable to assume that the effective *school* tax rate is 1.2 percent (45 percent of the 2.5 percent *total* tax rate). To generate $415 in school tax revenues and thereby support one child in the local schools, a housing unit would need to have a market value of $34,583 ($415 divided by .012), or roughly $35,000. (The required market value would be lower for elementary school students and higher for high school students, since the $415 is derived from a composite per student cost.)

The above computation assumes that the housing unit would generate enough school tax revenues to pay for the *entire* local tax share of educating one added child. But some of this added local tax burden falls upon nonresidential property. The Advisory Commission on Intergovernmental Relations compiled data concerning the share of commercial and industrial property in total locally assessed real property values within the suburbs of 27 large metropolitan areas for 1962 (*Metropolitan Fiscal Disparities*). The median share was about 18 percent. This share has probably risen since then because of rapid recent expansion of suburban industrial parks, shopping centers, and office space, so I arbitrarily assume that 25 percent of the increased local tax requirements caused by adding school children will fall upon nonresidential property. Thus the average added tax burden of one more schoolchild upon local housing in 1970 was about $311 (75 percent of $415). In order to generate added local school tax revenues of this amount, a new housing unit would require a market value of $25,917 ($311 divided by .012), or roughly $26,000.

7 *Statistical Abstract of the United States, 1971*, p. 34.

8 The key decisions have been in California (Serrano v. Priest), Texas, and New Jersey.

9 This conclusion is drawn from the in-depth analysis of housing subsidies presented in my *Federal Housing Subsidies: How Are They Working, and What Should We Do About Them?* (New York: Lexington Books, 1973). The specific data on indirect subsidies were taken from U.S., Congress, Joint Economic Committee, Staff Study, *The Economics of Federal Subsidy Programs* (Washington: U.S. Government Printing Office, January 11, 1972).

10 Data furnished by Henry Aaron from some special tabulations and from statistics set forth in his book, *Shelter and Subsidies* (Washington: Brookings Institution, 1972).

11 See Charles L. Schultze, *The Distribution of Farm Subsidies* (Washington: Brookings Institution, 1972).

12 See my *Who Are the Urban Poor?* p. 14.

13 *Statistical Abstract of the United States, 1971*, p. 317.

14 Concerning the impacts of transfer payments, see Christopher Green, *Negative Taxes and the Poverty Problem* (Washington: Brookings Institution, 1967), especially chap. 2. Concerning the relative tax burdens of different income groups, see Joseph A. Pechman, *The Rich, the Poor, and the Taxes They Pay*, reprint 168 (Washington: Brookings Institution, 1969).

15 Jencks, *Inequality*, p. 213.

CHAPTER 7

1   See Luigi Laurenti, *Property Values and Race* (Berkeley: University of California Press, 1960), and Erdman Palmore and John Howe, "Residential Integration and Property Values," *Social Problems* (Summer 1962).
2   See President's Commission on Law Enforcement and Administration of Justice, *The Challenge of Crime in a Free Society* (Washington: U.S. Government Printing Office, 1967), chap. 2, especially pp. 35 ff.
3   See Andrew M. Greeley and Peter H. Rossi, *The Education of Catholic Americans* (New York: Anchor Books, 1968), especially chap. 2.

CHAPTER 8

1   For an excellent discussion of the relationship of these two basic principles, see Robert A. Dahl, *A Preface to Democratic Theory* (Chicago: University of Chicago Press, 1956).

CHAPTER 9

1   The division of low-income households into two groups—mainstream poor and left-out poor—follows the thinking of Lee Rainwater, *Work, Well-Being and Family Life*.
2   Kenneth B. Clark, *Dark Ghetto* (New York: Harper Torchbooks, 1967), p. 49.
3   Robert C. Weaver, *The Urban Complex* (Garden City, N.Y.: Doubleday & Co., 1964), pp. 267, 30.
4   Ibid., p. 29.
5   Bureau of the Census, *Current Population Reports: Consumer Income*, ser. P-60, no. 77, May 7, 1971.
6   See Robert P. O'Reilly, *Racial and Social Class Isolation in the Schools* (New York: Praeger, 1970); Mosteller and Moynihan, *On Equality of Educational Opportunity*; and Nancy H. St. John, "Desegregation and Minority-Group Performance," *Review of Educational Research* 40, no. 1: 111–27.
7   This concept was originally developed by my father, James C. Downs, Jr. It is discussed at somewhat greater length in my

earlier article, "Alternative Futures for the American Ghetto," chap. 2 of my *Urban Problems and Prospects.*

8   Vernon E. Jordan, Jr., "Quota—The New Word Code," *New Crusader* 23, no. 17, September 30, 1972.

CHAPTER 10

1   Some observers have argued that requiring a "balance" between housing and jobs within 30 minutes' commuting time is too restrictive and that a longer time standard (say, one hour) should be used instead. Clearly, this would greatly extend the distance which any given housing unit could be from any given job and still be considered "accessible" to the person holding that job. I admit that using 30 minutes as the "limiting" commuting time is purely arbitrary and may even be too restrictive. That time is used in the text mainly to illustrate the basic concept involved rather than as a finally determined parameter of how that concept should be applied.

2   A recent study of an Ohio community employed a concept very similar to that proposed here. The authors considered a subarea to have a "balance" between housing and jobs if 50 percent of the workers employed there could find suitable housing within 17 minutes' commuting time. This formula is very similar to my own choice of 100 percent of the workers and 30 minutes' commuting time.

3   This practice is often ignored where school systems are trying to achieve—or avoid—some overall balance among students of different races or socioeconomic backgrounds, hence non-neighborhood-school assignment principles are frequently used in systems operating under racial desegregation plans. Nevertheless, in the vast majority of American school districts, the neighborhood-school principle is still dominant.

4   Up to now, federal courts have almost completely ignored *social-class* factors in developing plans for schools under court orders to desegregate racially. They have done so even though the evidence shows social-class differences are more important than racial differences in affecting equality of educational opportunity. Since there is no constitutionally grounded legal case against social-class discrimination like that against racial

discrimination, this issue has no legal standing in spite of its significant practical effects. I believe we should begin moving toward greater legal recognition of social-class and economic factors, as well as racial factors, as determinants of equality of opportunity.

5 The figures used in the text are based upon the following assumptions: (1) there are 2,000 students in the average urban high school; (2) about 7.8 percent of the district's total population is in the age group from 14 through 17; and (3) attendance at the high school equals 85 percent of the number of persons in that age group. In reality, both high school enrollments and populations in high school districts vary tremendously from place to place. But I believe these assumptions are adequate for the analysis in this book.

CHAPTER 11

1 John B. Lansing, Charles Wade Clifton, James N. Morgan, *New Homes and Poor People* (Ann Arbor, Mich.: Institute for Social Research, 1969), pp. 65–69.

2 These conditions have been explored in several studies of abandonment carried out for the Department of Housing and Urban Development. These studies are cited and discussed in Real Estate Research Corporation, *Preliminary Report: Possible Program for Counteracting Housing Abandonment* (Chicago: June 1971), an analysis also conducted for HUD.

3 This conclusion implies that recent efforts by environmentalist groups to stop additional development of new suburban housing could, if widely successful, prevent improvement of decaying neighborhoods in older big cities. If new housing construction around the peripheries of metropolitan areas is drastically slowed down, continued population growth in those areas could lead to renewed housing shortage conditions there. Housing shortages would in turn create "back-pressure" upon the supply of older housing units in decaying neighborhoods, raising rents and prices there. This reversal of recent trends would undoubtedly benefit the owners of those older housing units. But it would also make low-income households seeking decent housing worse off. Such a dramatic turn-around of recent housing-market developments

could occur even with lower future birth rates if environmentalist efforts to stop suburban growth are highly effective. This situation illustrates the potential conflicts of values and policies between those who place top social priority on improving the environment and those who place top social priority upon combating poverty and its many manifestations—including poor-quality housing. These relationships also show how easily people opposed to opening up the suburbs for primarily *social* reasons will be able to disguise those motives by seeming to advocate slower suburban development for primarily *environmental* reasons. There is some danger that "protecting the quality of the suburban environment" may become a code term for "keeping out low- and moderate-income households" among people who are really more interested in the latter than the former.

4   This conclusion means that decay containment might work if net new construction of housing everywhere in the metropolitan area was reduced drastically. As pointed out in the preceding note, just such a reduction is now being suggested by some environmentalists, who contend that continued peripheral development will "degrade the environment" around existing urban areas. But blocking new housing construction there could even further "degrade the environment" available to urban low-income households by raising the prices of housing available to them (see n. 3 above).

CHAPTER 12

1   I am indebted to Professor John Dunlop of Harvard University for emphasizing the key role of this principle in describing his successful wage-control negotiations with the building trades unions and the construction industry. He made this observation in a speech in Nassau in November 1972.

2   An excellent article presenting some current support for this conclusion is James Vorenberg, "The War on Crime: The First Five Years," *Atlantic Monthly*, May 1972, pp. 63–69.

CHAPTER 14

1   This tactic was proposed by Donald Canty, "Metropolity," *City* 6, no. 2 (March–April 1972): 29–44.

2   For an analysis of such principles, see Oscar Newman, *Defensible Space* (New York: Macmillan, 1972).

CHAPTER 15

1   This tactic has been proposed by Richard P. Burton in "The Suburban Crisis and Industrial Manpower Communities: A Social Planning Proposal," published as an Urban Institute Reprint in 1972.

Index